Charlie is Back

Author- Somnath S. Shobawane
(Junior Charlie)

BLUEROSE PUBLISHERS

India | U.K.

Copyright © Somnath S Shobawane 2024

All rights reserved by author. No part of this publication may be reproduced, stored in a retrieval system or transmitted in any form or by any means, electronic, mechanical, photocopying, recording or otherwise, without the prior permission of the author. Although every precaution has been taken to verify the accuracy of the information contained herein, the publisher assume no responsibility for any errors or omissions. No liability is assumed for damages that may result from the use of information contained within.

Blue Rose Publishers takes no responsibility for any damages, losses, or liabilities that may arise from the use or misuse of the information, products, or services provided in this publication.

For permissions requests or inquiries regarding this publication, please contact:

BLUEROSE PUBLISHERS
www.BlueRoseONE.com
info@bluerosepublishers.com
+91 8882 898 898
+4407342408967

ISBN: 978-93-6261-299-1

Cover design: Tahira
Typesetting: Tanya Raj Upadhyay

First Edition: July 2024

About the original Author and
His reflection about
Charlie Chaplin Superstar Comedian !

!!!CHARLIE IS BACK !!!

AS

!!! JR. CHARLIE!!!

Beautiful Life!!!
It is a collection of unforgettable moments!

Transliterated by -

MGM's Ex.JNEC *Prof. Arvind Kulkarni*
Snehsawali Care Centre,
Chatrapati Sambhajinagar (Aurangabad),
Maharashtra, India.

Email: kulkarniarvind2019@gmail.com
Cell phone No. 9284318183

My Conceptualization of the incomplete Mission begun
By Sir Charles Spencer Chaplin!

When I decided to devote myself to the Mission half-left
About my philosophy! (Junior Charlie)

तुम्हारा व्यवहार, स्वभाव, समर्पण एवं विनंम्रता तय करती है कि, संसार में तुम्हारी ये जंग,- कौन लढेगा?
आप स्वयं या आपकि तरफसे
यह संपूर्ण सृष्टी !

**The Butterfly Represents –
Faith, Transformation
And Acceptance to New Beginnings!**

Original Author
Somnath S. Swabhawane
Email: juniorcharli1980@gmail.com
Web Site: www.juniorcharlieindian.com
Cell Phone: +91-9595869370 (India)

Small goals turn into big victories.

1. Thank you to all those who paved the way,- for us to live more beautifully.
2. Don't strive to be well-known, strive to be worth knowing!!!
3. When Life hurts, Remember....this always..
It is the Bamboo that takes the drill,-
to become a flute!!!.

- Souls !That, get awakened in this
- Gruesome Path of Life,-Lives the Creative Mind!!!

What the original Author says

"Challenges!",-

Are....what make - life interesting.

- Overcoming them,- is what makes life meaningful !

And the Jr. Charlie (Pranav) says...

Of his Deity Lord Amarnath says

"Every day holds the possibility of a miracle!"

As a Prelude

to lifting a pen to write

Jr. Charlie Elaborates.

Life does humble you!

As you grow old, you stop chasing the big things and start valuing the little things more often.

Plenty of loneliness to ponder over those little things. Enough sleep, a good diet, long walks, and quality time spent with the loved ones.

Simplicity becomes the ultimate goal.

ABOUT CHARLIE - AS A MAN !

Sir Charles Spencer Chaplin was an English Comedy Actor, Film-Maker, and a composer who rose to fame in the Era of SILENT FILMS!

Charlie Chaplin became a world-wide Icon through his screen persona –"The Little Tramp!"

His career spanned over 75 years. Chaplin began performing at an early age- touring music halls and later working as a stage- actor and a comedian!

Today- we dive deep into the WORLD OF CHARLIE CHAPLIN, a renowned film figure-celebrated not just for his memorable silent performances,- but also for his thought provoking –quotes, interviews and the sound tracks; he went on to compose when finally 'Sound' did get introduced in 1927.

- Charlie Chaplin – whose primary medium of influencing the audience,-was silent film,- expressed profound thoughts through his written and spoken words,-such as

"Believe in yourself & You will be Unstoppable!"

Message that would guide you- as to the core nature of the great man.

"To the Beautiful Soul reading this,- I know life hasn't been easy, and it has been a struggle everyday to make it to the next.

Just remember that- no matter,- how many mountains you have to climb or how many storms you have had to endure, you will always have the strength to overcome life's challenges!"

PROLOGUE
!! Of Charlie Chaplin !!

Sir, Charles Spencer Chaplin - A legendary Figure was an English Comedy Actor, Filmmaker and a Composer –who rose to fame in that Glorious Era of **Silent Films**!

CHARLIE CHAPLIN became a word-wide Icon through his screen persona –"The Little Tramp!" Salient features of his Bio-data could,- be just ...

Born 16th April 1889, London, United Kingdom.

Died 25th December 1977, Manoir de Ban, Switzerland (Age 88 years).

His career spanned over 75 years,- of sharing His Wisdom with the masses.

Charlie Chaplin began performing at an early age- touring 'MUSIC HALLS' and later on, -working as a Stage- Actor and a Comedian!

> Today - we delve deep into the
> world of Charlie Chaplin,
> a renowned film figure-
> celebrated not just for his
> memorable silent performances
> but also for his thought-provoking –quotes!

- Chaplin –Whose primary medium - was **'silent'** films...specialised in expressing his profound thoughts through his written and spoken words. What this great soul implied through his life-travel-

"Difficulties in life do not come to destroy you, but to help you realise your hidden potential and power."

On His Quotes!

CHARLIE'S QUOTES ARE EXEMPLARY MASTER PIECES UNDERSCORING HIS INSIGHT !

> **Life is a miracle, and every breath we inhale is a gift from God!**

His equally fabulous quotes reveal his inner-self that rhymes with a classic sense of Humour. Some of them that strike my mind at this juncture.

1. "A day without laughter- is a day wasted!"
2. "My **'Pain'**-may turn out to be the reason for somebody's **'Laughter'**!
   But my **'laugh'** –must never be the reason of somebody's **pain**!"
3. Life! is a **Tragedy**–
   When seen in a **Close-up!** but a Comedy in long shot!

   (Charlie Chaplin life span lasted 88 years.)
4. Every experience that God gives us,
   Every person He puts into our lives-
   is the perfect preparation of the future..one that only He can see! And finally!
5. Life isn't about finding yourself,-Life is about creating yourself!

Posts that flash on the Social Media are from of its columns that do bring out the Wisdom of the Literatuerers,- who took time to comment on the Great Man, and similar persona!

"Never stop learning, because life never stops teaching and at the same time keep alone educating the right ways of tacking the obstacles – that come – in his travel."

(1) "Sometimes you do get- what you want, and or at other times, one does get a lesson pertaining to real meaning implied in usage of terms such as Patience, Timing, Alignment, Empathy, Faith, Perseverance, Humility, Trust, Awareness, Resistance, Purpose, Clarity! Grief, Beauty and Life itself!
Either way – you win"
    ..... Brianna West

(2) "MIRROR is my best friend because when I do cry,- it never laughs!"
    ..... Charlie Chaplin.

(3) *रिश्ते चंदन कि तरह रखने चाहिये चाहे टूकडे हजार भी हो जाये, पर सुगंध ना जाये !*
    ...शायरा दिपीका.

(4) रखलो आईने हजार
तसल्ली के लिए
पर सच के लिए तो,
आँखे ही मिलानी पडेगी।
खुदसे भी और ...
खुदा से भी ...

(5) Good quotes can inspire
Deep thoughts about life
so I can navigate my life better.
What I am today,
is the result
of my own thoughts!"

(6)   "It is a disciplined mind that brings happiness!"....
(7)   "Happy times come and go.
    But the memories stay forever!"...

!!!CHARLIE IS BACK!!!

"Charlie is Back! is,- in fact a highly captivating novel"

This year happens to be

A 135th Memorial Day of that Superstar

The Comedian-

- An Ever-smiling Original Author-Composer Director

SIR CHARLES SPENCER CHAPLIN.

This Manuscript opens itself with scenes from the yester year Videos accompanied by the

AUDIO BOOK.

Certain paths that we come across to tread,- during this travel named LIFE,- we have to walk –all alone -by ourselves -all that distance without any co-travellers and that too just,- believing in oneself! and with the courage streaming from within!

There does come a momentous time in this travel –"**Life**" when one has to walk away from all the drama that is manifesting itself around you and you are perhaps being forced to move away from the very people who created it. It's much better to get surrounded with people who are remaining perfectly focussed on the 'good',- one comes across. God's sole direction stands limited to this dictum - "Love the people who treat you right, and pay for more souls who don't. 'Falling down' during the life travel is also a part of the life bestowed on you by the deities- but getting up back and attempt yet again is what true living calls upon.

To those co-travellers in this travel of Jr. Charlie Foundation,

As 'one' you speak, you touch, you think, you feel,- and all this all the time,

I hear it! I feel it! I know it! I sense it!

> But love the inner music being played all the time!
> One that is Soul –deep and embedded,-
> deep within one's inner-self and
> that itself triggers a feel of eternity in its content!
> "I met you",-
> And instantly –everything made a sense to me..
> I realised ...let me tell you-as I mused –walking onwards,
> Every mistake I committed in this travel to –date.
> The paths that I did take...
> the places where I had lived...
> the people I had met ...
> and the decisions I had made...
> All those things did lead me back to you!
> All the wrong turns,-
> I had taken earlier-
> seemed to transform themselves into the right ones,-
> when they finally
> did take me back all the way to you!

> So meaningful and an eternal music then...
> kept on getting played in the mind
> while travelling all alone in this universe
> or ...*Bramhand* (Universe/Milkiway) the way we call it!

That soul-touching music kept on being played

Universe on its part,- watching all this struggle... and us,-

Unaware of..what Destiny has in its store

It was then that the magnifying of what ...

Life had bestowed – it slowly unfolded that content as we moved on ... of a

Love –'Soul-Deep!'- Embeded and Eternal !

The Junior Charlie was now in full flow explaining to me about what made him think of Charlie Chaplin Missionary Zeal as a work,-left half done.

"Referring some notebooks and perhaps a bit to the Google Store, the artist from this typically Rural Mode of living,- that had come his way so far,- and the raw way in which he had been brought up– replied anything... yet again from a lecture he had heard recently. He maintained that, Charlie Chaplin did make us realise the existence and sanctity of these four fundamental aspects that should be attended to – in our life travel."

(1) In this world- There is nothing that is a permanent one! Even the problems we tackle / face are never permanent in that sense.

(2) I do move around a lot in rain- because – It is only then that no one else can get to see the tears in my eyes.

(3) The day when we do not laugh at all,- is one of the most wasted days.

(4) "As to those six doctors – that matter in physical fitness of oneself – Sun, Rest, Exercise, Food, Self-respect and friend circle, that I had mentioned earlier. If we obey their restrictions and do avail of a really happy life lived, - then in a spirit of beautiful words... "If you see the Moon- then invariably you'd see the real Beauty of God! If you see the Sun in a proper perspective, you will sense the Real Power of God! And if you do see into the mirror opposite yourself, then you would be able to see the most beautiful creation of God!"

And that is why have faith now that
We all are mere travellers
In the travel named LIFE
and God is after all, our Sole Travel Agent,-
the one who booked our this journey.
The Yatra !
As we Indians call it (as I would call it)
and whatsoever would now be manifesting
in front of us.
It is 'He' who has planned it all!
If you then do believe in it
it is then that you'll realise
that 'Life' is only
such a journey!
And so, today- let us all enjoy

and live this life with joy
Resumed yet again
What exactly will be tomorrow itself like
We do not know,- whereto it will lead us also not known
and that's why, my dear ones, do understand this
that our attitude towards life today
should be totally turned to
This Reality! Playing true! To that Tune ! The one,-
Eternity plays on and on!

An impressive locale of **Amarnath**
Striking a Soul deep, one that's Embedded Deep
within one self, - That eternal
music being played on and on...

"Amarnath Heritage Journey !"

Chapter-2:

People start the final leg of their this holistic Amarnath Yatra riding the 'Pittus (local Kashmiri lingo word- Khacchars)' provided by local contractors. And the pilgrimage commences with a shout of Jay Amarnath!, Jay Baba Burfani!, Jay Amarnath!-the kind of cheers we hear all the time on such occasions. The entire area reverberates by this shout of cheers and an atmosphere of total devotion all around is being experienced. (In the background – Songs and Bhajans- all in the Bhaktiras Pattern of Music can be seen –Songs and Bhajans sung by the pilgrims can be heard as well).

Pranav has got his leg wounded,- all of a sudden. So he pulls out the shoe worn by him,-all by himself. In a way- that wound had happened because of an injury sometime back itself. But it had not got yet cured. Just a Bandage was tied around the wound.

Road now starts becoming rockier and rockier. As the road keeps on becoming more and more difficult to walk,–it becomes quite clear by his facial expressions,- that he was sensing a possibility of rain starting anytime– but he kept on going despite the unbearable pain being quite acute because of the wound that had not yet got cured.

Pilgrims now get off the shoulders of these carriers hired by then under a Khacchar contract and offer to pay him the already prefixed amount and after paying, they start whispering amongst themselves. Just then the voice of one of the pilgrims is heard and is recognised by Pranav. Getting interested as to what was being spoken, -Pranav then speaks out to that particular pilgrim.

"Sir, do give me your phone number. I will certainly come to your Maharashtra for some work /job. We really are in dire need of some regular work and regular income. Here, we do have work,- but only during this Pilgrimage Season.

For the rest of year- there is no work at all.

No work!-So no income! But yet our family has to be taken care of. Even when we negotiated our this *khacchar* contract with you, Sir, you had already promised me that you will get me some kind of a regular income-in the film line if I come to your Maharashtra and do a job there.

The Pilgrims laugh at this talk of his and scribble a number on the backside of a photograph of **Sai Baba** look- alike and gave him what, in fact-was just a fake number. Having given the number, one of them speaks- to him,-telling him, "You come directly to Mumbai. Anybody will guide you to the film city- Mumbai is in Maharashtra itself and the moment you reach the gates of film city, you do call me up at this phone number. That's all you have to do. Then, rest assured that your entire work there,-would be completely taken care of.""And yes, don't forget giving me a call that, you have reached Mumbai film City Gate safely!"Pranav promptly answered, "Yes sir! Certainly sir! I will give you a call. Nice of you all,- to have thought of everything. Jay Baba Burfani – Jay Baba Burfani! Jai Sainath ! Jai Sainath!"

By the time Pranav finished his, this talk, the pilgrims had already left on their return journey- without waiting anymore as it was now getting dark.

Pranav now tired- looking at the pilgrims returning to their native places. Switches on an old radio,-an old-time companion of his!.

A Hindi Audio clip... just sounds as though reflecting on Pranav's inner feelings. The words flow beautifully in tune with the late evening atmosphere.

The beautiful male voice comes out of it. As if it was Pranav himself singing to himself! He continues muttering to himself –his own misery as a family head in that valley..

बिना किसी मंजिल के

और

देखियेगा-कि मंजिल तो दूर कहीं

खडी थी

वो खूद ही इक लम्बीसी डगर बनी थी।

इन रास्तोसे जुडसी गई थी

कुछ यादें हमारी

और

अब महसूस हो रहा था जैसे

वो यादे ही खडी है वहाँ – गवाह बनके।

क्या पता और कब
उन्हे वक्त भी मिलेगा या नही
हमारे बारें में कुछ सोचने का
और शायद वह शुभ घडी आ भी जाए कभी
हम यूँ ही –वहीं कहीं पडे रहे होंगे
बस एक राख बनकर ।
या किसी कबर में दफनाये गये होंगे।

- अनामिक

The nearest English meaning of these philosophically rendered lines... that strikes me would read like this. The lyrics, in fact are born out of a deep introspection and I am attempting to submit these lines for the benefit of Non-Hindi readers.

Nearest English Meaning-

Oh! We do seem to be moving, walking on and on ....
without even a destination in our mind...
Let me tell you and the *'destination'* itself,-
was there standing all the time
all alone by itself!

And yes – my memories are linked with that road....
And somehow I keep sensing –deep within
That these memories,- too got up stuck there itself
Now standing –as mere witnesses to
Our this never ending walk...
Along the path laid out by the destiny!

Who knows when at all, they will even find time
And that too merely to think,
about us! Our plight!
Those memories of our feeling
....so lost! as if a mirage
When at all they might find time-
Lord Himself also unaware!
We might at that time,
Be either,-there itself
Lying somewhere nearby,
On the road....
Either dead or burnt down to ashes!
Or having got buried – in some graveyard nearby!
And the road keeps on moving,– all alone
It now without any traveller.

(Music now over – Shot returns to Pranav still eyeing the path... taken by Pilgrims to return to their states.)

Pranav, in the meantime terribly pained by the reopened leg –wounds, – and the blood flowing out- leg now,-in an awful condition now,- but yet he drags himself to a temple nearby – and with lot of expectations – he attempts to pray desperately for the Deity's blessing to let him complete the assignment safely and the words come stammering out of him.... in broken English, something that he had picked up in all these years of accompanying the pilgrims in this holistic pilgrimage.

Pranav now calls out in pain, praying all the time.

"Amarnathji, Amarnathji – After all,-

You are our only all– rounder!! The only Gaurdian Amarnathji, I do bring, every devotee of yours to you– Desirous of coming to your place... for the Holy Darshan.

And he...Gets all his wishes fulfilled within just a moment,

And to help those devotees to reach you,

I do everything that is in my power....

And that too,- in a spirit of service to you ..

Because of your own grace and blessings

Devotees achieve what they seek and

When they do get all this,-in just one trip In all their life till now, all this just to seek your support and help...and, by your grace They do get relieved of all the troubles That have been troubling them! I now want you to tell me Amarnathji, What crime I have done- "What fault of mine, my lord, makes me feel that That I am not being taken care of...By your own goodselves. Lord – just look at my this sight of wounded flesh....My feet are stained with blood, But yet I have been dragging myself.

And I am still bringing...

All your devotees to your door...

Seeking your *Darshan*...

And what do I get in all this hard work,-

Just a few rupees given by them,- for the services rendered
And, this birth too,- that I have got, I do know
Has been given to me by you only.
Now in these circumstances,
Do tell me how will I be able,-
Survive till next Pilgrimage Season ?
To maintain myself and my family,-
Serving you and your devotees in so low an income?
Tell me, how at all,
I can take good care of my wife and children?
In this miserly Income? During this wait
for the next Pilgrimage season to begin!

My dear God-
The supreme Divine Deity that you are
But now when I look to you ....
Only as my last source of support–
And strength that you bestowed on us
Saying so, and tears wetting his eyes fully,
He rests his head on the floor in front of the idol
And then shows God once again
That piece of paper-
With the scribbled phone number
Showing it to God,-
 He keeps it carefully once again in his dress.

Having sought the blessings of Lord Amarnath yet again.

(*The close-up shot near the Amarnath Cave is in light mode!*)
(*In the scene, of the Darshan of the Amarnath Deity looking at his devotee! and it looks as if the Lord Himself is now blessing this staunch devotee of his.*)

Scene cut.

✦ ········· ✦

Chapter -3

The Amarnath Pilgrimage season is now over

Shops – That entire suburb,- with all the shops in it,-

had been opened specially for the visiting pilgrims..

are seen being shut down,–

They will now remain closed till the arrival of next season.

The scenario is now of a vacated locale. The lights too have now got dimmed. The number of pilgrims and the local people seen moving around are getting reduced fast... as most of them,-have already left by now.

Some seem to be still in the process of packing-up and leaving –as it is more or less now the sunset time.

Life –now- has drowned into a quietness.

It shall remain so... for the interim period.

Camera moves all over the place–

What gets now seen,-it is a scene of just few characters loitering around and apart from these people- not many are seen!

That the soul motive of all these incoming migrants pouring from literally all parts of India- all of them sharing – just that one DREAM that this DREAM CITY does help them fulfil their DREAM cherished for so long,- would be getting transformed into Reality in just a short time.

This "Desire for fame- that too worldwide fame!" and that this fame should also be accompanied by abundant riches to own best of luxurious amenities that they couldn't even otherwise imagine. All of them- DREAM MERCHANTS! Looking out for abundance is the very crux of all this travel by these strugglers.

And lot many locals –attempting to encash on their this mad-hunt for fame and wealth by these innocent, ignorant migrants and all of them–hopeful and optimistic. They are people drawn from literally all streams of society with a total ignorance or understanding of what essentially is their limited knowledge and limited skills- yet aspiring for a ***Status / Star Identities*** for beyond their capacities and all aspiring to become Superstars, Artists, Actors, Musicians, Composers, Directors and what not!

All driven by that one craze!

Seeking that Worldwide Fame!

Getting involved in an awfully unfair a struggle of resources !!

And desires- beyond their capacities !!

And on becoming failures- losing their own identities-

Now becoming somewhat like just living, corpses devoid of Any self confidence –in the flow of time!

Getting shrunk in size and spirit from humans to mere ants / cockroaches level!

And
What to say,- they do opt
to cut off all their links connections
With their own families
And all this misery, is in a way their own self-created mess
in that wild desire of asserting themselves, and proving to
themselves, their own self-capabilities.
That single urge! The only Motivation
Search for New Identity!
Desire to rule the world
Visualizing for themselves a
"From Rags to Riches" story
Rags keep sticking on
Riches- nowhere secured
Beggars –Paupers
Are now their new identities.
Lost in the flow of Rivers
Dragged by the pull of water flow
Eyes that outshone all,- while dreaming
Now dull and unwilling to see around
These Lost Souls – searching
Escape routes! raking up
Suicidal thoughts in mind
The thoughts rocking deep inside!

While the Audio clip plays on.....

Camera pictures the wild rush of the busy Mumbai Metro life.

The thousands of people travelling in the local trains,

hanging on for the locals to stop, attempting to get down using the door....

At the station they seek....

Confused and Stunned faces aghast!

(Scene Cut!)

◆ ········· ◆

Chapter-4

An online conference is going on the screen.

All the Invitees to the Conference are seated – perfectly in a professional way.

All the invitees look to be highly professional people and are – in their Professional Businessmen Attire !All are now looking at the screen.

The Noted Director of Film City itself, also a celebrity in his own right, is now on the screen, being seen by the Invitees. The Invitees seem to be satisfied with the seating arrangements mode- for a priority discussion as to the current day status of an extremely confidential project now nearing completion –before its being commissioned. It is about briefing all of them as to an update of both the till-date achievements and further plans.

The noted Director, I referred to above– is about to commence his address- to this meet of All –India Renowned Professionals- drawn from a variety of backgrounds– each one of them–seems to be highly resourceful, well –connected and at this time-seem to be quite attentive as the film-world's Master –Producer

Director Nanarao commences to address the meeting. The hall has been magnificently furnished with all requisite professional tools like mikes etc. for the exchange of Professional Opinions- immediately after the VIP (referred to) above finishes his much awaited presentation.

The situation now is that the main speaker will be shortly begin addressing all the professionals- now comfortably seated at their allotted space – each of them with a support official standing just behind him to be available on call. The convention does understand- that while the speaker is addressing- there will be no verbal interaction simultaneously going on amongst themselves. A total silence has been instructed as–no objections or suggestions are welcome while the main address is in full flow. Restrictions like these are, in away something like assuming acceptance and understand doubly in view of the importance of the topic and ensure that, such instructions are accepted by these invitees as well.

The situation- in which all these persons are finding themselves... today is,-one of grimness of the situation and as such this meeting is one of a vital update about the crisis being faced. Choice available as to pursuance of the project and decision as to some decisive action seeking the consensus amongst the invitees–following what now was being expected as the Chairman's highly professional talk.

✦ ········ ➔

Chapter-5

Director producer Nanarao begins his Address:-

Good Morning, friends!

I am quite confident in saying at the very outset of this informal meeting about the progress done hereto, problems faced and that are still being taken care of, - to some extent and as to the unavoidable further steps,- in ensuring that the vital project is progressing properly. That you all,- are doing well both in your chosen professions and also health-wise,-at the same time, is what my personal concern about you as our Esteemed Associates,- may kindly be taken as a part of the business records of this meet.

This particular problem that has been playing on our mind since past few months has been making us feel a bit restless and also apprehensive too. Whatever we had at that time conceived as a dependable alternative / a solution in that direction,- we have to report,- having achieved a considerable progress.

The alternative, -quite a creative one – in reality is a completing "AUTOMATIC MAKE –UP Machine" and giving it the final touches. The Machine has been conceived by all of us and it makes me proud to tell you all that, -that this typical kind of a very special machine that we all had dreamed about,- has now got fabricated– It is consisting of lot many Subassemblies – that can fit one another– when the machine is to be installed at a local or in a permanent special hall like this specially made to suit all the imagined activities and programming those activities in a perfect sequence that could not go wrong.

This is an announcement that the machine, so visualised by the Top Creative People -backed by "gifted scientists and technocrats"-, has now become ready for its first trial –We have been, to a large extent quite successful in importing all the requisite subassemblies - under the guise of "waste – equipment" so as to facilitate an inspection-free import. We now claim success in getting it correctly assembled in our this very Studio.

So as of today- this consignment– completely assembled from all those imported parts, sub- assemblies– received in a properly done despatch schedule–in accordance of priority, that is followed in a foolproof assembling sequence under the guidance of a Foreign Technocrat– expert at the assembling and commissioning. The machine is now almost ready for usage and getting prepared to become perfectly operative.

Model Machine Ready for final test and commissioning

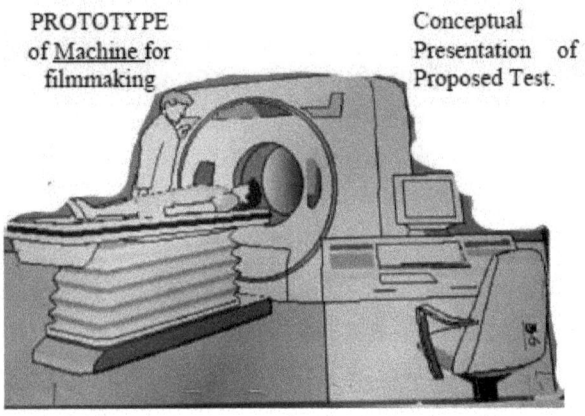

PROTOTYPE of Machine for filmmaking

Conceptual Presentation of Proposed Test.

"This success that, has been achieved would not have been possible without your cooperation and the requisite support extended as a top priority matter. That's how we could manage to bring such a machine into our Bharat by getting it broken down into various parts. Importing the completely ready machine itself was not possible for reasons explained to you and so the various subcomponents that go into the assembling of machine,-had to be imported just as **spare parts**. Now we shall have to reassemble them,-here in India and the first test of the assembled machine would have to be conducted to our satisfaction as to the output quality.

After this successfully conducted first test and if this experiment about which,-we all are highly expectant, then we should be able to do any film made anywhere in world– not taking months / years but in fact- the time taken to produce would stand reduced to as low as few minutes to few hours' range and because of this possibility, we would stand to slash the production costs and recover whatever monetary investment we have done both in the conception and the making of this innovative Machine. Our investment, you all are aware has run into lot many Crores of Rupees.

We now, propose to get this machine duly commissioned for getting the first film proposed to be produced. Work in that direction of a Movie with an intelligent content is expected to commence shortly after the commissioning of this machine, (which is our first step) is achieved.

Now I will opt for a straight talk with you all.

Investment in this prototype machine that has been incurred to date in importing it to India– in all that,- as our Equity Share is more than your all investment done to date and so I declare that, the very first movie,-that will be made by this machine, would be by us of course with the help of this machine- That production will shortly commence and I will personally ensure that it is done pretty fast under my supervision.The very first film that has been proposed to be done,-With help of this machine, It is with immense pleasure that...

I am announcing the Name of that 'Magnificent Movie'.

The name of the very first movie is about the
World-Famous Comedian Superstar, Charlie- Chaplin
And is captioned as......

!!CHARLIE IS BACK !!

It was a round of scenarios witnessed during and after the second world war- when people numbering well over crores– belonging to both the warring parties- had got killed. Lot many of them, are now merely living corpses moving hither– thither not knowing what to do.

Scenario witnessed everywhere were drought with fear and the calm that prevailed all around was of a quietness that was purely a horror-created one. It truly was of what could be called as one of grief and tears all around the world!

And it was precisely in this period that Charlie Chaplin took a decision that he was intent on going to devoting his entire remaining life to his sole concept, make the entire world – laugh once again.

He has already created that image of himself known all over the world as "The Little Tramp!" the trendsetting role. We then took a decision of making up of this character once again coming alive and also decided to opt for making up the entire range of all the scripts as well -as our usual and admired production features. So, a massive **Remake Programme** was now on our mind.

So with this aim in our mind and while working continuously in that stated direction, we decided to go in for online for pooling together all the scripts that featured Charlie Chaplin and his various presentations and then to feed all the collected data into this our own machine to enable us to develop a Memory Base of surplus various scripts and shots creating a Memory Base afresh, has been on our mind all the time.

And now we wish to see if we can come across some artist who could even be uneducated in the context of Film-Making and we place him in a Typical Sleeping Posture and be fed into this Machine and attempt to transfer all the above collected "Memory Base" busy into that artist's mindset. Then we should theoretically be able to reduce substantially the production duration. Whether we can slash it down from otherwise 7/8 months duration to merely a time duration of just 7/8 hours and succeed in coming up with an output which would be up to the same quality level and in keeping up with our production standards–without incurring any loss–in the intensity of personified gimmicks of *Charlie Chaplin*,-original actor or in any of his mannerisms–as displayed in his earlier movies. That kind of gentleman is what has been an unseen guideline in our coming up with such a thrilling concept.

So, stressing once again, I wish to state that, with this outlined mindset of ours-we shall now be concentrating on our efforts to come up with or find an artist– who could be totally uneducated (in the sense of theatre/filmmaking), someone with a totally blank memory as to the famous Charlie Chaplin endeavours to date– either on or off the stage, off the screen because of his not having seen or heard anything about them- we propose to push him inside the Memory Base that we have got made, once the actor is inside the specially invented machine ready for receiving **that** proposed **memory transfer**.

We, of course, shall be taking every precaution that, the persons' or the Artist's mental frame work doesn't get affected nor he incurs any loss of his present mental abilities.

Well, as you all are fully professional mindset and business people and so you will be able to understand that we cannot indulge in such as experimentation that would be in an "open to all!"Atmosphere – especially more so, because we are in no position to get such a permission in *Bharat (India)* as even our Hollywood Associate Producers, do not stand any chance of getting such a permission in their country.

As to Bollywood, it would simply be unable to come to our aid and help us out of this predicament.

So... it all amounts- to what appears to be a bit Dirty from legal angles

Dirty - all this is certainly –seemingly so for the superficial ones but yet the lure of the massive business and the likely impact of savings on film production economy that might flow in –as an output of this risk being taken up by all of us jointly in this daring experimentation.

Ladies and gentlemen, that in fact, is our greatest-temptation and the lure that drives us to risk (that might not be appreciated by lawmakers) - that preciously sums up what one would comment on this interaction amongst the powerful minds that have assembled here today.

And today we have reached such a stage that all the components and the sub assembles have been assembled,- ensuring various amenities in it that are necessary too and so have been provided simultaneously and is now totally ready for the final experiment. This kind of machine can be used in Hollywood production as well but even there, this Human Rights Acts people would forbid allotting any such permission and block the experimentation. So we all have reached this stage of a thought process that–if we do find such an individual who has no connections at all, someone who has no successors nor dependents, someone who doesn't have any official identity of his own, we therefore, so put out a search for such a person – and if at all – our this experiment does succeed-(with his cooperation and wilful participation)- to our desired expectation levels- we,- in lieu of his service rendered by him, the cooperation he would be extending, he would be rewarded with a reasonable payment and help him get a fresh official identity as well–and if at all, the experiment somehow does fail despite the best of our efforts, care- then you can take it from me that the novice– Actor would have bid us a permanent goodbye.

(Close-Up Shot of the machine on next page clarifies the way the proposed Artist would be pushed into the Special Machine styled.. "ARTIST–MAKER MACHINE!"- equipment with all the needed scientific equipment preparing the person now in a sleeping poster to absorb all the data into his blank mind- along with all pertinent data as to costume wear – body language of that Celebrity Actor Director !).

This actor would be paid a reasonable token in the form of an advance token payment to cover his immediate present needs and would be so stated in an official contract of his consenting to do all that is required in this experimentation. It would definitely be an historic achievement made possible by this his volunteering for the ROLE, for which he has been given complete idea of the risks to be faced during the production. This is being done as a step in taking a precaution as a protection against some untoward legal complications in the event of this project becoming failure despite all the care exercised.

And yes today being 29th Feb. – A strange amazing day that presents itself once every four years is also in a way a day of unlocked potential. Let us, guys, then opt to use this very day to attempt something totally extraordinary and take a chance to shape up a totally different character and create a miraculously afresh the same pattern of the professional mindset of the departed superstar out of all this intelligent effort while launching the world's first movie by totally surrogate a modality afresh.

That very much the same pattern of yet another Actor Reincarnated – by bestowing into his mind,– The details of carefully built-up Memory base of that Superstar comedian of yester years- ***Charlie Chaplin.*** Come to think of it- this effort of ours could even be thought of –as an innovative attempt at Surrogacy – restricted to the Acting Arena! And that too just the acting talent !

Search was on far such a willing Artist and an uneducated one without any cognizable background or successors, to worry about, one who is willing no barter his participation with an offer of a subsequent fresh official identity and of course the fame that would invariably follow and yes a considerable amount as a monetary contribution to cover up his lifetime needs of his own sustenance.

✦ ·········· ✦

Chapter 6

During this long travel from Kashmir to Mumbai,

Pranav Raj–Suddenly remembered that the day he would be reaching Mumbai was in fact the 29th of February- One that comes up just once every four years. It was on such a date- that he would be presenting himself at the Gate to the Film city of Mumbai- that had promised him a good job there. In a way, every day is of just 24 hours duration. Day that awakens –presenting one a chance to become someone – organisable enough – in displaying some skill- that is embedded in him / her and – is signalling that it is now time to parade one's own performance, Pranav Raj had been lost in these kind of thoughts all through this journey.

With that same piece playing on again and again in his mind,- Pranav Raj got down on a platform that presented itself and put his foot on it, most lovingly and then rested his head on that Mumbai Railway Station Platform floor,- all the time chanting the name of his Deity and saying "Jay Amarnathji!" Kissing the photographs of Burfani Baba, he said, "Barfani Baba, finally I did reach Mumbai- have reached this huge metropolitan town. He then kept on looking at the phone number given by his Mumbai friends on the backside of the photo, that did look like being one of Shirdi Sai-Baba. He was looking so adoringly again and again at that number. That the people walking around him felt that, he must have been drinking all the time and so is lost in that elated mood.

He then sought one or two of the people walking past him and asked very politely, "Bro,- Here in this city, where is that film city? Can you tell me how to go to it?" Looking at all his get up in the Kashmiri Dress and taking pleasure in the interaction, that person jokingly said, "Hey Babu! Have you come to Mumbai for working in films?"

All that,-he now had with him was that just one phone number – hurriedly written on the backside of the photo of His Burfani Baba! It was merely on the strength of having just that one number,- Pranav had reached the Film City Gate.

Now he had absolutely no idea as to what Deities upstairs had written,- on his forehead? All that he now saw there – was just a Watchman,– standing right in front of him and now was, in fact now asking him, "Do tell me which set it is that you wish to go? and my dear Bro, for opening this door to enter, you better produce at least your own ID.

"Saheb! This is the number those people had given it to me. It is on their say that, I finally managed to reach here. Do please ring up this number. It is these people who had told me,- to come for work to Mumbai and had said, give us a ring on this number, from the *Filmcity* gate and we will come there immediately and pick you up! So sir, right from *Amarnath Dham* I have journeyed to Mumbai- now that our season there,- is over- for some work that had been promised to me here, and with the blessings of Lord Amarnathji, I have finally reached here just today.

Watchman / Chowkidar once again now stared at this fellow standing in front of him and then he said, "There is no such kind of phone numbers like this here. That's why you will not be able to get inside the studio. But you can stand and wait here outside and if at all there really is some work, I will give you a call to come up."

It was in this condition,- that the poor fellow got stranded for the next 24 hours. It was already night. Hunger was on the rise. But yet, there was no sign of anybody coming in to look for him. He started becoming restless and was simply unable to make out as to what to do exactly? Pranav was too confused and restless as well but still stood,-kept standing there only and in all this time,- just waiting for someone to come and hoping that he does gets some work to begin with.

All the night, that was how it had been passing – Pranav got totally lost in all kind of thoughts- that had begun to crowd his mind... He then chose to think of one thought that struck him that was worth much more of a ponder.

'Name and 'Recognition'– or call it as an 'Identity Craze'- if you so wish – but these should be an outcome of someone's very own – hard earned one– attained by literally pouring one's very own inner-self into that effort – the hard work being put in.

Respecting all,- is really a very good thing but desire to live in self respect – that alone matters a lot-in this exercise of creating an identity of one's own – which allows one to stand out – even in a crowd.

A co-traveller had come out with some kind of a saying of his own- while travelling in the some bogie as he was in that train journey– Kashmir to Mumbai.

He did recollect, not the very words that the gist of what had been hinted at – was something- that did make a sincere listener– pretty introspective.

Pranav – in his inner self- now repeated that thought yet again to himself – that was aptly befitting what he now really sensed, felt- about the 'humaneness' that was getting unfolded around himself. Strange people- totally different ones- had been looking at his typical Kashmiri Attire bit amused at his broken Hindi/ English dialogues-but accompanied by lovely smiles blooming beautifully on their lips,- and so typically a *Kashmiri* style.

The quote had centered around this summation.

God! Upstairs has given all –

an aptitude to laugh at things going beserk.

One shouldn't lose that ability ever,- to smile.

Let the laugh- the smile bloom on your lips!

Well, you see- by talking lovingly – even to strangers...

Your own property doesn't get wasted!

It really is true –

That a human being gets born in every home,

But the grave reality is that-

It is this "Humaneness!"-

That gets born in just ...

A few homes and places.

While going on muttering like this to himself –

Pranav dozes off into a totally tired –

Much awaited sleep – on an empty stomach –
Beside that Film City Gate
That claims to be a gateway to..
Name Fame and what not..
Hoping all the time for a –
far better tomorrow ...
That might....Rain success on his,- this wander!

*****

Chapter - 7

Stars Appearing in the Opening Shots of the Movie "CHARLIE IS BACK!"

Assistant Cameraman
'Soch!' Media Staff.

Kartiki Madam
(Upcoming famous reporter 'Soch' Media)

An upcoming famous T.V. Reporter / Anchor Kartiki is seen lost in a mood of her very own. Just 20-22 years of age- beautifully dressed,- eyes radiating naughtiness and sharp intelligence– very probing eyes that could not be missed by any onlooker,- speaks little but when she does, she ensures driving her point home effectively.

Today, she seems to be out on a search – for both – her channel "***Soch***!" and is on a look out for a specious – *masala* story line for her own Daily as well.

Waiting and waiting for her signals,– alongside her is that very sharp minded Assistant Cameraman– with his camera ready for any shots – that the lady might ask for,-he stands there,- watching the scenario around,- wondering as to what the lady might be thinking of – at this location.

Kartiki is totally lost in that atmosphere around,- raking in that excellent Sea-shore scenario around her this morning and while she was lost in that mood -her phone rang up.

"Hey!' Madam Kartiki! Where in the world are you?

Bloody hell! you seem to be having a gala time on Marine Drive Sea- shore? And if I am right – Right now you must have got

yourself into that famed *shayarana* mood of yours! And you,- my dear one,– as a change must have begun to hum some old Hindi Melodious Film song of yesteryears – befitting that locale.

"My dear Kartiki – Would you now snap back to work – mode

Pay attention to the call of duty also –

You and your that,- dammed artistic mind.

My dear girl – if I don't get any news –
Befitting that, Page 8- do tell me what am I to do ?
Yours news *Maal-Masala,* so appealing to the readers
Has still not yet reached my table
for that page 3,-the Special Page of yours!
That has made you famous-

Now it is better if you do get yourself moving ...
And send me some news pretty fast.
And hey, let me be very straight forward,- about this...
If you cannot comply with this demand or fail to meet the deadline..
You can very well be sure
That you will now be absolutely free..
Therefore to go to your own home!
And bid us while on your way,- a final goodbye!"
(The caller disconnects without waiting for her response.)
Saying all this in what seemed to be a "no more nonsense!
Mode- The caller had cut of the line,- on his own!
No more non-sense will be tolerated–

Seemed to be the clear –cut message from the Channel Authorities.

And that 'daring' shown by the dammed guy, totally insolent behaviour..

To do a prompt disconnection – in that rough style..

Without even, waiting for a reply – that was pretty insulting!

Annoyed Kartiki (Short for Kartiki Madam) to no end.

Kartiki Madam annoyed with disturbance that broke the chain of her thoughts as to work at hand started,- muttering to herself-

"This on-demand: Journalism Work – looks so damn attractive from a far away distance– but in reality it is quite a hell. Working under this 'deadline' pressure all the time! Do the guys that now are well known – names,-do they do such things and put imaginary news that would reflect in the TRP ratings. Well, let's first get back to reality around here. That damn message certainly meant business. If now, I cannot come up with some real *Maal –Masala* news as they call it- the TRP tonight might slip downward and even bring down that very precious Advertisement Revenue–so vital to keep the operations going on. And all this, just so that they keep on getting their attractive monthly packages and we the poor guys doing the field work – we are made to run wildly after getting such news or go on searching for them all the day,- or if so required we have to invent even some fake News to suit the Editorial Board.

She continued her this rabbling as the cameraman stood beside – listening to her this charade, her outburst. She then said to herself, "All those – who did practice journalism in the days of **Lokmanya Tilak**- were honestly great fellows, who really did some real good stuff of genuine journalism work. In those days, there was no such need for any such kind of wild hunts for the "*Maal Masala*" type or "Hanky-Panky" kind of news and now take a look at us. We the present day journalists are overburdened with such crazy demands and stupendous expectations! We, honestly have no inkling whatsoever of the reality –we cannot even be sure about which would be the last bit of news given by us would be getting published – with the due credit to all our efforts and hard work put in-Well, let that all go! To her Asst. she then turned and said, "Well friend! Let's begin our works, we shall try as much running around as we can,- for as much time as is possible while we are yet on their Pay-roll.

And yes, till then – why at all keep bothering about whether we shall be on duty tomorrow or not?

Come to think of it– I had read this somewhere... of a wonderful NEWS
"Joy / Happiness is all – just an illusion –
Something we keep searching for -
Sadness is one such experience
That in these days is in plenty,
Yet in this life-
It's only those people
Who really became successful.
Only those having a full confidence in themselves!"

Kartiki gets ready to leave; but is still disturbed..
By that call- She starts saying to herself,
"Now 'what's there' to show?
What at all I got -by meeting you?
Bit of restlessness and lot more peace,
Little uneasiness and lots of patience!
Little involvement and lot of confusion
Bit of Bitterness and lots of sweet talk!
Little naughtiness and lot of delicacy
Little bit of enmity as well and lots of love!

The day- when I do not get to talk to you
That day passes on silently-an uneventful day!"
On a straight wide long path –
Long one and right in front of me,
Someone like a friend-
Walking quietly alongside me-
Somewhat like a friend –
His upset face –
Silent though,
Yet showing all,
Is unhappiness –
Depressed as well?
And finally! when we do meet face to face.
(Starts to laugh out at the turn!)
This gory day – turning its back to me – says
While tickling me at the same time,
Tell me! My dear friend! How are you feeling now?
On a straight wide long path-
The one right in front of me
Someone like a close-friend,- that road
Too-walking quietly alongside me
Like a friend –equally upset-
Its face showing all the turmoil within!
Unhappy- silent and
So Depressed as well!
And finally – when we do meet face to face
And then that gloomy day –suddenly
Begins to laugh aloud at my this muse-

It is then that this gloomy day to
It tickles me to no end-
Yet asking me as if
Tell me- my dear friend!
How are you today-
Silence raining all around me-
Me with a smile on my lips-
Moving on and on
Thankful or thankless –
That feel of mine!"

Chapter -8

"One who meditates as a Devotee of Lord Siva
He will do real good work!"

A courier man was going right in front of Pranav for making some delivery. A packet of that Courier Man,- got dropped on the road. Pranav then called out aloud to that Courier Man,

"Hey! you! Bhaisaheb!" Calling him once again loudly, he then picked up that packet from the road and handed it ever to be Courier Man, who smiled while thanking him.

Just then that,- very moment....

The famed Director Producer Nanarao came to that very gate to collect a parcel that had come to him from that same Courier Person. It was then that his attention went to the shabbily dressed Pranav and so, he then enquired with the watchman –"Who is this person?"

Watchman –then told him all very clearly.

"What to tell you sir? Right from morning itself, this fellow has been making me feel awfully restless. On one side he is moving around with a photograph of a *Saibaba* lookalike and on the backside of that photograph – there is some phone number hastily scribbled. He is showing that Sai Baba's photo to all and says that person is the one who has done this role of *Saibaba* and that particular person is very much inside the studio and you please let me go inside to meet that actor who did this role!"

"Now sir, you do please tell me,-which among these hundreds of Artists that work here,- is the one who has acted the role of *Saibaba*? How can one find that particular artist and what's more that this phone number,-the one given by that said Artist is totally a wrong one. In all probability this fellow must have given that artist a lot of trouble and that person must have attempted to get rid of this troublesome fellow and so; purposefully must have given him this totally fake number,-which is wrong one !"

Listening to all this –Shri. Nanarao, the famous Director got totally surprised. Yet he asked, "But this man? Where does he come from?"

"Saheb, he says he has come from the deep valleys of Jammu- Kashmir- He is one of those who attend to the comfort of visiting pilgrims who come to Amarnath and it is Lord Amarnath – who takes good care of him because of the service he renders to the visiting pilgrims....during rest of the year.

This is what he told me just today afternoon. Throughout the last night he looked totally troubled and so I took pity on him because he seemed to have had not eaten anything. So, I gave him my own Tiffin box to him and he quickly gobbled it all, that which was in that box. He truly had been starved totally because of that long tiring journey and not finding the people here who had asked him to come here and contact them on this number on reaching here.

"He simply has nobody of his own here. No one! - No one to care about him. What he carries with him is just these photographs and behind that photo a number scribbled by some stranger- who cannot be found/ located.

Nanarao: (Surprised at the revelation) What in the world, are you telling me? Just a photo and the number- The one that is totally fake and he then comes all the way from Kashmir trusting that fellow who gave him just this number?

Nanarao did muse for a while, then continued and spoke on.

"Well! Come on! Neither, is that number wrong nor fake and neither he has reached a wrong address."

"But what is really wonderful is the mere fact, - that this fellow,-just on basis of faith in that photo, he came all the way to Mumbai right from Amarnath."

"That is what,- is truly great. This trust in his Deity and the confidence he had about the phone number given to him."

"And all this thing,- rather such thing can happen only in case of a truly needy person,- he alone can do all this. And what's more *Sainath Maharaj's* Doctrine was actually "faith and patience", "*Shradha Aur Saboori*" Trust about God and trust accompanied by a patience – based on just this much as his capital this guy did reach this place- Well! Now, what you do? – You send him to my office. I will talk with him and I will leave instructions with my watchman also. If such and such a person does come inside,-bring him to me."

'Now first get him bathed properly and arrange for his dinner and his stay here for tonight as well." Saying so,

Nanarao departed. Watchman stands looking at the backside of Nanarao and mutters to himself- "Bloody Hell" Nanarao never cares for anybody whatever the pressure. But in this case- about this fellow there really must be something that is interesting in all this.

Scene cut (Burfani Baba/Sai Baba, snap – and the famous Kawwali hailing Saibaba starts being played in the background.)

Chapter - 9

As instructed by Nanarao– Pranav then went to the gate of Nanarao's famous Studio, part of the Film City.

The watchman there,-welcomes him and respectfully takes him inside and at the same time points out to Pranav – the room. By a wonderful coincidence in that room, there is an excellent photograph of Lord Amarnath. Seeing that photo of Amarnathji as it was similar to the one that was in his cave. Pranav becomes wonderstruck. He gets thrilled by the thought-that his Deity is here also,- to look after him, to take care of him. For a moment he feels dazed and becomes stunned for a while. He respectfully bows in front of that photograph and it is at that moment itself, the watchman calls for him from behind and says, "Bhaiyya get your hands washed. I have kept some clothes for you to wear, get fresh and wear them and then you can have meals."

"Nanarao shall be talking with you after some time!"

Listening to all that was being said by the watchman, Pranav standing still in front of that photograph of Lord Amarnath- tears swelled in his eyes and not saying even one word -he folded his hands (in front of the watchman now watching him and lifting that photo? Photo!"-in that his typical Kashmiri lingo, and began to cry,-sitting straight away on the ground right there.

What is going to happen? That is not known.

What is now to be done? That too he doesn't know.

What to do now? That also is not clear to him.

"Life" therefore transforms itself into a big question mark at that very moment lulling him into total silence.

Tears flowing down the cheek.

Nanarao mutters something to himself....

Perhaps saying what a timing to find...

"The kind of Artist,-we really wanted for the trial"- he seemed to be muttering to himself at the stroke of luck unthought of !

Chapter-10

After a short while, Pranav hears of a sound-of his room's door now opening- and a voice calls out to him- from outside the door only,-saying, "Saheb has called you to the office."

What follows, is a conversation between Pranav and Nanarao, in Nanarao's room. In the room, just the two of them begin to talk to each other

Pranav is confused- uneasy and sweating as well.

Pranav then tells Nanarao,- the entire story of his life upto this moment,- without leaving any important detail and relates to him how he has incurred lot many debts while maintaining his family on the meagre income source, and that what he has is the only one little bit of money saved from what the Pilgrims give during the *yatra* days.

There is no other source of income apart from this seasonal earning -but one has to keep incurring expenses all though the year. He does tell everything in detail, about the pitiable state he is in and speaks of his family back home. He doesn't know now what to do if there is no work!

Family will now certainly be expecting some money to survive and by the time he ends his recital of the fright he is in, Nanarao assures him, that he will give some money to him, the next day and tells Pranav about how to send money to his village in Kashmir on priority.

Nanarao tells him that, he can consider this money as part advance for the work to be done by him. Nanarao then added in a quiet tone, "I have total confidence in the machine that is awaiting its first trial!"

Pranav – retired,- after getting some money to send to his family and by the assurance that his own personal needs of shelter and meals will be taken care of by Nanarao himself and the watchman – relaxes a bit but speaks out to Nanarao saheb.

"What to do, Saheb? We are the poor people!

We are worth 'nothing' when we are alive.

Such is our poverty and if at all, things do not improve then we have to commit suicide on our own, and then no one even bothers!"

So, instead of all that, I have that much of faith in my God Amarnath and as He is showing me the right path. Right from this path, now shown by him. I shall follow whatever,- He asks me to do. I am taking this money in His name and well let's go and see what He wants me to do now.

I don't really have any idea of what He has kept in store for me, but anyway before I die someday, I will at least now get to know that I have tried whatever I could for my family...

When I would be practically dead for all others. "

Chapter - 11

Photographs of the AUTOMATIC MAKE-UP machine into which Pranav would be pushed while in sleeping position on the stretcher.

While all this talk and conversation was going on in the room between Pranav and Nanarao,-lot of supportive activity had begun in the studio already.

Shot:

Around the Machine a cleaning work is going on, as some scientists and technicians are rechecking the machines from technical point of view ensuring that all the requisite parameters requisite for proper experimentation are well set, and in order.

Nanarao is standing there personally guiding all the process and is available for the briefing to be taken by all technical people as to their having assured themselves that all is set perfectly for the most challenging experimentation in the field of film-making. Success in this experiment would totally throw the hither to,-known economic parameters of higher productivity as to filmmaking modalities, "topsy-turvy" leading to slashing lead time in the making of an international level of filmmaking and obliviously reflect in a massive slashing of production costs in future and the Film Industry- related Economy will get a further impetus because of reduced costs/ capital outlay.

Whether Pranav's mind can withstand the sudden influx of vast input of all of the Charlie's movies to date beginning right from the Silent Era to the days of his feature films, his interview, his world tours. All of these inputs would create a huge memory base as to mannerisms of the late but original Charlie Chaplin. Materials such as dresses and costumes used by that Charlie etc. had been pooled together by the side of the machine with the idea that after Charlie is pushed in with all these support material and once the downloading of the input data is totally complete, Pranav should be able to step out of the machine room duly dressed as original Charlie-back in action mode. So all these costumes he used,- the walking stick, baggy pants, oversize shoes etc. etc. had also been carefully sanitized and had been kept ready for usage.

Pranav in the meanwhile is looking at all these preparations that have been going on around him. He seems to be deeply lost in his own thoughts.

"I had engraved...

Some beautiful moments!

In my memory lane..

Wondering about whither to this life is leading me!

But then those alphabets...

Scribbled so hastily on the mind screen

Glowed for a while –

But got diffused in no time –

In that void space that engulfed me!

Machine– that one-perhaps,

Might as well turn out to be a Beautiful Coffin-

Whatever it might be...

But bestowed so lovingly by that Lord Amarnath

I shall soon be settling in that -

Hoping I will finally find that evasive peace

Not beauty, nor money or the status I dreamt of

My mind perhaps might shut itself

Out to this world that surrounds me

It's the spirit that I keep looking out....

For some Charlie....

And people around-

All caught up in preparing that machine

For the final lap-

My mind now getting raided by the moments

Lived by some Charlie- of yesteryears

who – in his new identity –now being borrowed from me...

- promises me to look after my family that,-
- I shall be leaving behind.

All this could it be a fraud ?

Untrue / A Curse/ Total confusion?

That's what – I sense deep within this silence! A dormant feer!

Silence..is a far better an option

When words do fail one…

And then…yes,

I forgot – me-myself – I am from Kashmir

We there – all of us

So fluent in this language

They all call it as " THE LANGUAGE OF SILENCE ! "

We grew up there-

Watching, unnecessary massacres all around…

And I now stand here

Watching yet another murder... this time of my own..

My identity being hijacked by a dead man

By his devotees led by a Director

for some shot- They all call as

MOVIE OF ALL TIMES!

Chapter-12

Nanarao gets a Thumbs Up...
Signal from the Leader of all the technical staff.
He now steps forward for the press briefing..
"Namaste friends, Namaste to all of you!
Today, we are on the verge…
Of a fantastic invention here in our own country Bharat."
"This invention shall create massive economic changes,
Apart from incurring huge profits to our companies,
And I assure you all that...
All the representatives of our sister concerns
Who have chipped in both money and participation
In all the decision making...
With their active roles in this joint travel of ours,-

Their future too will be taken care by us.
I will promise bright future for all the participants in this fantasy format of an effort that would affect not just the psyche but ensuring that the memories of Dead Celebrities can also be stored live with all their those im-memorable

speeches and Lovable Mannerisms and would be with us once again in a modified incarnation and be able to redeliver their wonderful creations against current day backdrop. Memories will also be receiving a makeup for the time gone by,-ever since their death and the time when we attempt to rekindle them.

This kind of activating a retrieval of all those unforgettable moments to update the present day generations and set new standards for the future generations. In a way, in fact we are attempting to help God in ensuring a continuation of the Charisma of some of the historic personalities who lived on this planet.

"This all,-has been possible because of the vital cooperation of you all and we extend our very best wishes to all those Directors/ Producers / Financers - who are watching this video conference, now live."

"We are getting to be busy with our work."

"Do ensure that this subject matter remains shrouded in a veil of secrecy for some more time while we polish out the schematic machine. That could be first of a new generation of machines, prototype of a mind- set, "Memory-house transfer!"–making it up alive yet again entirely in retrieval, the history of vital characters lost to the History of the mankind.

We shall be looking forward to you all joining us, alongwith this working team for a Gala party celebrating the Master Invention made possible by an unimagined Team-Work spreading over few continents as well venturing into that rarely understood field of the Psyches of fabulous Human Brains who influenced the world history!

The Title of this first ever effort would be....

"CHARLIE IS BACK!!!"

Kartiki was fully attentive as the media briefing neared its end.

For some unknown reason it came as a surprise even to her, but yet her mind recalled a Pythagoras quote.

"The oldest– the shortest words we know of! – are "Yes" and "No",- are those which require the most in-depth thought prior to their usage.

So true! She said to herself watching the action that was going on right in front of her!

And now it was the turn of the Foreigner Machine Scientist who had come specially for the installation and commissioning.

Chapter-13

The foreigner Machine Scientist,-who had come to help in the installation and commissioning of the specially assembled machine.... was trying to make the Indian scientists understand the technology apart from stressing the pressure on him to return to America as he had simply mentioned, "The purpose of visit" as tourism and nothing more." Because of the reason so stated, he said, it will not be possible for me to stay here for too long a time.

So as such, he said that, "it would be far better for them to understand the program being explained to them and let him leave early so as to reach his own country in the laid-down return-schedule. Whatever steps, I am saying have got to be followed in toto or else I will not be responsible for whatever might happen in case you make any mistakes. Follow the computer language program step by step as explained and I can only express a hope,- that you have all understood the procedure to work as an Associate with your team. That is what I expect from this interaction amongst us. Thank you all for the patient hearing to my lecture- a short talk!"

Chapter-14

Machine – Make up machine- is now under a shroud of lighting put on.

On its desktop, a photograph of Charlie Chaplin is seen.

On the outside, Charlie's costume, shoes, coat etc. are hung in a specially fabricated hanger. The makeup material has not been put there as the machine itself was expected to ensure the total makeup of the artist in its entirety.

All the people including staff and scientists are now fully silent.

The atmosphere in the studio machine room is totally silent one!

From the machine, various musical sounds seem to be coming out as a background is getting created for the word- Go!

Pranav is standing there- totally calm and quiet,- wondering about whether he would live / die as the program gets ready to be now put on. He is praying from his heart,- seeking blessings of his Burfani Baba! Neither crying nor smiling at all. In a totally helping mood and temperament, he lies on the machine as directed and is lulled into a perfect silence. Heartbeats of all those watching the activity keeps on beating loudly, increasing the Heartbeats of the Producer Director Nanarao too. Now his Heartbeats too, could be heard on the sensitive mike. – in front of him.

Dhak... Dhak...! Dhak...!

One big sound comes out of the machine and the machine announces –

"Mission Successful"

All programs have got set in the mind of Pranav!

As instructed specially the,- **"Charlie is Back!!"** script also and the make-up instructions as to enhance effectiveness of the body language of the Actor. Validation period limit set for just 15 days as directed by the Producer Director Project on for just the coming fifteen days. Activation of software installed satisfactorily over!"

Pranav is now seen stepping very slowly out of that machine.

He is wearing the costume by his own hands. An entirely different kind of smile is now on his face! Original Pranav is now lost, left in the machine itself and Yes! Ladies and Gentlemen!

The original *Charlie Chaplin* – The famous actor director now playing his role in **"Charlie is Back"** has stepped outside the machine for shooting to begin,-immediately.

The schedule that otherwise would have taken well over 90 days would have to be completed in just on an 8 hour schedule. This entire effort is apart from importing acting skills is also directed at compressing the lead time required to complete the work in just 8 hours,-different places, locations, all over the studio. All those present,-are now moving fast along with, the new **_Charlie Chaplin_** a manifestation by Pranav (*directed by the Director or by the computer program already loaded*) is seen also moving stepwise a perfectly synchronized motion picture which is under protection of a secrecy unheard of.

Stunned TV Channel Artists, and reporters all are intensely watching History being created. A live manifestation of the dead Charlie Chaplin in a fantastic style and in a way, a crazy brainwave of Nanarao is getting enacted, - and manifested effectively.

And all of this is being enacted as fast..,

That everyone has begun to sweat but,

Charlie was unwilling to stop at any juncture, the reason being,

Is that,-he is now no more the rural actor Pranav...

But in his memory what has been fed as a data,-

He now has transformed himself into that brainchild of Nanarao's Charlie. And now the Role of this Character of Charlie, That had been enacted in this episode is approaching an end.

Almost all are on this verge of displaying an unlimited joy,

Gleeful on the demonstration of the fact,

Machine that had got assembled had worked beautifully!

As per the laid down program by Indian Engineers.

A great step in the Art of Film making

And while all have got immersed in what seemed to be a pure bliss,

Charlie goes back nearer to the machine.

Director Nanarao announced,

"All programme loaded in the Artist mindset have been executed perfectly. All scenes too are satisfactorily- over."

"Now for you all- an important suggestion. That the scenes that we shot today, the selfies taken here at this locale should not go viral at any cost. A **must caution command** as to maintain total silence. None of are you are to even whisper about whatever is happening here. Till the time, our 'make' is not completed fully to our satisfaction, and a perfect compliance as to the standard expected- till that point we cannot speak of how we used this machine. The online members too are requested in the same way as to the total secrecy that is to be maintained. Today's this shooting that would, otherwise, have taken 90 days and has been smartly done in just 8 working hours! Just imagine the economic advantage achieved. In all probability, the entire investments made in this machine would be recovered by the end of the completion of the very first Movie, itself.

Ganpathi Bappa Moriya!
Sadguru Sainath Maharaj ki Jay!
Jay Baba Barfani!

And the moment the Actor's clothes got removed, tears started flowing out from Pranav's eyes in an uncontrolled way and while still weeping silently as he gets into the machine once again. And the Indian scientist standing near the machine,- in that enthusiasm and excitement,- presses the wrong button. And while Pranav was still inside the machine, there took place a sparking un-thought of.

Everyone stood shocked,-wondering at what really happened? That was the worry on every face there, the sound heard was as if still some fireworks had been getting burst inside and almost –immediately the sound coming out of the machine finally stopped. Pranav stepped out from the machine yet again but what really was fabulous was that, the one who stepped out now was not our poor Pranav. He had not stepped out. The Neo-Charlie Chaplin-as just the one who came out was still that loaded Pranav. The new Charlie Chaplin as just the Charlie we knew from the Audio Video world of yester years and years gone by... was moving around.

Now the guy simply doesn't recognise anyone, no one at all seemed to even attempt to reason out with him. There was no such "work order" inserted into his brain to sound in case of such an eventuality. Pranav that had stepped out was the wrong mix. When this guy had been leaving the machine, the man who stepped out was now not Pranav nor Charlie. He had now become a Mix –Personality,- an unplanned Character living lives of two men and that just one out of them had actually stepped out,- the others perhaps still in a **slip mode**.

After having stepped out of the machine, he glanced at all those around him just not recognising them at all. He drank the water that had fallen below just near the machine. He rushed around the studio and even before Nanarao could make out what he was really upto, he jumped out using a pole that was lying nearby and with its help, got himself thrown out in the Jungle on the hindside of the studio.

Nanarao was by,-now shocked and he shouted to all those around him...

"Hey! You stupid guys, take out all your vehicles and see if that guy has fallen in the forest behind our studio. If he is dead bring him back duly packed into the studio once again. In no situation he shouldn't enter the market place that is nearby. That place stupid guys, you all now rush, rush out fast!

What are you looking all? At my face like that! First thing get that, Charlie fellow back in the studio or else you all can be sure that we are all finished! Totally 'dead' or 'alive'! Get that guy back into the studio! No one should get to ever know that we all did was an experiment on him without any legal permission !!"

Chapter-15

One small township!

Pranav trapped amidst the tree–plantation nearby. Seeing all this Nature's beauty,-that's all around, he is in a confusion state of mind.

He is not speaking to anyone– nor making any sound.

He gets down from those trees.

While getting down,- his foot falls on a tender worm moving-

He, then suddenly –moves his leg away from that worm that had got hurt by him and with lot of feelings- he tried to fondle that worm lovingly, caresses it affectionately and keeps on saying all the time, "Oh! I am sorry, I am really so sorry!"

He then starts embracing the trees also,-as if they too were his real friends,- whom he was meeting after a long time. And it started to look as if,- those trees had also begun to chat with him in their lingo,-having recognized him and as an old friend of theirs visiting them and at the same time,- wholeheartedly welcoming him.

While walking amongst the trees- he came across a small footpath that goes on to meet a little wider pathway. In all this world that was around him, he simply– is not aware of what had really happened to him? What he exactly did for the sake of earning money, that too he wasn't aware; what could be the danger awaiting him at the very next step/turn. This innocent–ignorant character–somehow managed to reach that slightly wider path. Having reached that path– he sees that what seemed to him,-as a School Trip–carrying lot many children in a specially arranged bus for a Picnic in the thick forestry that was around,– with few teachers accompanying them. The staff member- teachers who were accompanying those children on their this picnic day- thought that this Artist fellow might have come there as a "Surprise Element!" And so, they took the Bus near that Artist- and all the children got down from the bus and had a great time of merry– making, and jumping around– playing all kinds of joyous games, enjoying all kinds of funny dances with this unknown Artist. And despite all those wild games and laughter going all around him- he simply didn't even ask anything to them nor even spoke to them- But he did participate whole heartedly in that dancing around! They all had their tiffin food,-brought along with them,- which they shared- amongst themselves and other staff members and this Artist Charlie. Charlie then – in his own typical fun-evoking styles,-fed their own food to them, only making them open their mouths and made them gulp down,-the food so served by him. The entire scenario was one of pure happiness and joy all around. So as such and it was in this way that this our Charlie took care of the hungry 'Pranav' who was inside him. Such a conclusion could be drawn by those who knew what really was happening.

While all this was going on and on- it was now time for the boys to return to their homes. All the kids now boarded the bus once again and along with them- our own Charlie too, got himself into that bus. The accompanying teachers felt that perhaps this artist wished to go to some nearest Railway station and so they did not object to his boarding the bus. Let him come along –was all that now they felt. What the confused teachers had really thought of him was that, this was an artist from the nearby Film City and perhaps– it might be that our School Authorities who must have hired his services for a day. So, with that thought in mind- those teachers and kids,- joyfully put a Rs.500 note in his pocket. But Pranav, was the present Charlie who knew nothing about this prevailing money aspect. What he knew and what he was conversant with was just Love! Love and Love only! And it was now that the 'Real' Charlie's journey began in right earnest.

Charlie had now really come back.

Yes, guys, you are right!**"Charlie is Back!!!"**
"Of life-
As I went on,- penning this
Beautiful script's English version!
Something I recollected-
"May be I am different than most,
But I do not see people in my life
As part of a game!
If I am your friend,
I am loyal until my last breath
And if I love you,
It is until my last beat!"

-Anonymous.

Jr. Charlie – in an informed chat,-said about his admiration for the Original Charlie Chaplin,- in this way-

"Distance never separates two hearts that really care,

for our memories span over the miles and

within seconds-we are there.

But whenever I start feeling sad,

because I miss you,

I remind myself of how lucky I am

To have someone – so special to miss"

Cherry Off !

(An English Poet of Repute!).

Chapter-16

Nanarao, by now,-had become thoroughly troubled, upset and at the same time quite exhausted. He had been talking with all the gangsters on the phone.

One team of these gangsters did cross this Bus that carried Charlie but the gangsters had no idea that Charlie could be in that very bus. They in fact – passed alongside the forestry – towards the forest to search out Charlie there – and so- in this way, Charlie got once again saved from these dangerous hands,- hands of those hooligans sent by Nanarao.

Charlie– does get down near the railway station and promptly – In no time, lot many people.... now begin to gather around him. They get promptly busy taking selfies with Charlie. And while they are still busy in taking those selfies –a local train arrives–one which was headed for C.S.M.T. (Chatrapati Shivaji Maharaj Terminal). While photos were being taken, Charlie sees this local and simply is unable to overcome the temptation to board that train and Charlie in fact,-does board the train.

The public, co-travellers in that local, in which Charlie had boarded the train, do get overjoyed to see the Superstar Charlie travelling with them. They all then begin to get selfies taken with Charlie displaying a wide grin – in that costume of his. Some of them had already begun to give him something to eat– some even started putting some money in his pockets,- some gave him biscuits- some put chocolate like eateries in his pocket and some gave him money as well. Charlie becomes quite happy at these gestures of gifts. Charlie, presently in an **unscripted** kind of position. There is absolutely, at this moment no script at all which had been loaded in his mind. But his body is dressed in the Charlie Make-up. He does not even know if he can speak anything at all, could he understand anything at all? He might not be knowing even this! Does he have any consciousness or awareness at all?

He happens to be just an innocent one,- who doesn't carry any guilt and so very ignorant as well. His fault is just this one- He is not guilty of anything. It is in this role,-that he happily goes upto C.S.T. At the C.S.T. he meets the T.C.

The T.C. instead of asking him about his ticket- happily gets made,-a selfie of his own this with Charlie and bids him a Bye!

Charlie – then much the same way... steps out of the C.S.T. In the outside atmosphere now, almost all the public start getting their photographs done with him-once again the selfies etc. and he tries to find his way out from where he was deep within that mob. Police comes out in his aid and tell him to move slowly,-holding on to the railings. He then passed thru Hutatma Gatway, Kulaba and gets an unexpected pleasure of a Boat–ride. All the people have been thinking that he is a VIP who has come for a pleasure –trip –to Mumbai and with lot of respect for him- try to have photos taken of themselves..with the Saheb- with that Internationally Acclaimed Charlie Chaplin in person !

There is same kind of a special enthusiasm amongst them to share the pleasure of their being in the VIP's company. Public is having the pleasure of a boat-ride. All those striving for the selfies with the VIP are busily tied up at the same time,-in the activity of making it a news item, Charlie too, on his part - now avails this happy chance of a pleasure ride in the boat and straight away goes on with them to the Elephanta Caves.

On the other side- Nanarao's people– do come-up to the Gateway. But they do not find Charlie towards either Gateway or Kulaba side- because Charlie –at that time was already inside the Elephanta Caves and so, yet once again Charlie gets saved from Nanarao's notorious gangsters.

Chapter-17

Sunset is about to take place

Sun now setting down for the day

The last boat – by now coloured totally rosy,-because of flowers and garlands offered to Charlie by the Co-Travellers in the boat,-would now be heading for the Gateway,- on its return journey.

That evening...

Would it turn out to be the last evening for our Pranav/Charlie?

That's the thought in my mind right now.

In this destined night–whether Charlie gets trapped by those gangsters is something that only GOD knows!

From Kulaba end- these gangsters have now begun for reaching the Elephanta Caves as a last resort to search out Charlie. They seemed to have thought that 'Charlie' would be still in that small village there on that island itself and it would turn out far easier in finishing him off there itself!

The Elephanta Caves is a Tourism Attraction of repute in Mumbai. There exists a small village too near the caves and that is totally surrounded by the sea. So, they thought amongst themselves,-having finished him there itself once for all–we can easily throw him into the deep waters of the Sea and the work given by Nanarao to us would have been taken care of or at the most- we can plan to kidnap that guy from there and take him right to Nanarao and hand him over. These were the thoughts – kind of what they had come up as ideas – in their own planning. I recollected a famous Charlie quote at this juncture.

Charlie Quote- *"I remain just one thing, and one thing only, and that's I am simply a clown. It places me on a far higher plane than any politician! "-* ***Charlie Chaplin.***

Chapter-18

The one whom God extends this protection personally–who at all can kill that person! Pranav or Charlie,- who so ever he might be now .. for me it is just a **Pranav–Charlie**... he now departs by the last Boat.

And just then...

The boat of Gangsters reaches Elephanta Caves in their own boat there – But then.. they don't know that, they had come too late once again.

For yet another time,- the gangsters and Charlie give each other a miss! – and Charlie –straightaway leaves for the Gateway.

The Gangsters now get totally busy in trying to search out Charlie in that Elephanta Caves, nearby areas and the sole village on the island.

They simply do not get any trace or have any doubt that Charlie might have already left for Gateway--by the last boat- that very day.

And they,-so instead of rushing back to Colaba- they get busy in searching for Charlie– in that lone village,-that is in the Elephanta Island,- near those caves.

On other side- Charlie gets down at the Gateway-

He then starts drifting... as per his whims with people following him.

From there – he reaches Marine Drive by a walk...

Goes on slowly towards the Hutama Chowk-

Enjoying the sight of the commoners walking on the road, where night life of Mumbai is now warming up...

Lights- Music –Glamour- Dance- Clubs...

And he himself adding the clown like acts to the immense pleasure of the upcoming younger generation also seeking night life pleasures.

Now becoming Charlie Chaplin yet again in an extremely happy mood,

Making the youngsters go ga-ga at his mannerisms–

with those facial expressions-

making everyone burst out...

laughing out a loud creating a festive atmosphere.

His own sense of music –

The steps, he takes in those baggy shoes

Waving in that, very typical way of his own gimmick famous walking stick happily, at all those around

Sharing... wide grins with all of them-

The commoners getting just thrilled–

Becoming an evergreen darling...for one and all..

Of that crazy young generation...going ga-ga on his show..

Sending them to Waves of Laughter... so difficult to control..

He is continuously moving on the road

Taking such Hilarious Short Joy- Spots,-

With that immemorable grin of his, so attractive

And finally reaches,- in this mood...

Locations of Sidhivinayak first....

Bows down before that Deity..

Getting all the Devotees pleased..immensely-

With his boyish simplicity and a wild- rush

For his autographs– selfies with him, being the craze...

Now being continuously taken.

Then he moves on directly to Haji Masjid-

Thrilling everyone...at that locale as well !

And then moves onwards to Mumba Devi

Getting a Darshan there as well!

He has no ideas as to where to keep on going

moving along the road the way it takes him..

And following him,- are those people,

Who are responding to his this drift,- to nowhere in particular..

And it is in this way that our dear Charlie –

Inches his way and

By sheer coincidence–

Finally reaches once again to the Dadar Railway station!

And there, awaiting for them all...

Is the ***Vande Bharat*** Train...

Reaches there– people staring at him..

Just because of people's affection putting him there-

He somehow reached there and once again...

Selfies taken by the people,-

Dazed by his this sudden and unexpected an appearance...

While walking to the station,-

He calmly goes on showering smiles all around!.

He simply has no ticket- Nor any destination

Doesn't know where to go –

He is showered so much love by the Public –

That his drinks, eateries etc. care is all attended to,

By the new radiant faces surrounding him, specially the youth...

Pure bliss- they all seemed to be sensing...

Being seen with the one and only one-

The Superstar Comedian of Yesteryears ....**Charlie Chaplin!**

What all was happening around,

He could not understand any of it.

He in that happy mood,-

Not thinking of anything nor knowing,-

What all this is that is happening around him,

And he without speaking to anybody- and straight away

Boarded that Vande Bharat Train awaiting at....

Dadar Railway Station.

The great man now –comes to know-

Train is headed for Shirdi Sainath Maharaj Mandir.

It was as if Saibaba Himself had issued a personal call for this artist,

Sat in the train with people around him focusing their camera on him.

The Railway staff – Technician staff all are extremely overjoyed.

Happy and instead of asking him for the ticket-

They happily serve him food and drinks...

And also have their photographs taken with him

And in this way...

Charlie then begins to entertain,-

All the co-passengers in the train-

Driving them to go, ga–ga over...

The hilarious and so expressive a face of Charlie ...

Making mimes and living the moments

That figured in everyday life of all!

And while his entertainment has reached quite a peak,

It is in that very train...

Saibaba's famous *Qawali* song

Started getting played- adding to the joy of all.

On that song and stepping in tune with it- Charlie gets them all lost in joy totally and succeeds in making all this crowd lose itself in the mood of that song. It is for this kind of a journey that the train is there....

For Journey to Shirdi!

Charlie unaware though –is now,

On way to that Sainath Darshan

To present himself in front of that Sainath idol..

Co-passengers hail in one voice,

"Sadguru Sainath Maharaj Ki Jay!"

Chapter-19

Nanarao thoroughly angered by now- firing all those gangsters of his-

for their failure to search out Charlie,–

who had been engaged in that wild run around..

Manhunt on so big a scale,-ever undertaken by them..

And at the same time- in the Media

A whirlwind of news items started pouring in...

Captioned under seemingly the same headline

"Charlie is Back!!!" "Charlie is Back!!!"

"An actor today played the immemorable role of the Yesteryear Superstar Comedian- Charlie Chaplin in moving-

Right from the morning itself–

from entertaining the School-going children,

Right to old age people–footpathers–

Along the Gateway–Colaba– Haji Ali, Mumba Devi- Siddhivinayak temple, Dadar Railway Station, but no one really knows who actually is this actor? A mystery, - Media on the Lookout! **Who is he?** "

So all the citizens and public have been asking the Media about who is it?

Media, on its part is trying to locate that Artist –

But this Artist has been missing since morning –

He was in Mumbai –

But overnight –where at all he has now gone?

No one knows.

No one even is aware about from where he does really come from?

For this actor – who so ever it might be,- could be either ***Pranav*** or could be perhaps ***Charlie...***

Long Ques- begin to start forming in no time. People waiting for hours.

Just on the basis of rumours, that...

Charlie is likely to be here on his vacation. Those Ques...

Very long ones have started

Lining up right now everywhere

On lookout for this actor all over Mumbai.

But where at all is this Charlie? Pranav ? or who so ever? That Actor is!

They all say-"!!!**Charlie is Back!!!**"

But where is this Charlie now?

A search for this Charlie is also going on – by the Mumbai Gangsters and on other side by the Media. It seems as if the gangsters seem to have a plot to kill Charlie without even knowing who he actually is–

Public support–on so large a scale for this Artist makes it awfully difficult for the gangsters to catch Charlie and kill him.

Will the gangsters get Charlie?

Or..Whether the Media will be able to lay its hands first on this Charlie.

News by Kartiki- of Soch Media!

Made the First Breaking News on TV on 'Soch' Media Channel.

-"Charlie is Back!" Kartiki with her stupendous News !

"Who is Charlie?"

"Charlie on yet another mission?"

"Charlie claimed to be a psychic case"

"Case of a psychopath... retarded by some mishap / accident?"

"Charlie – An anonymous Actor... "

"From Bollywood film world? Confusion abounds!"

Movie Mafia shocked by such loose talks!

Who wants to murder Charlie? For What?

Be on watch out with Cameraman.

This is Kartiki of 'Soch' Media.... News abuzz !

Search on for the mysterious Actor!

◆ ········ ◆

Chapter-21

Charlie – In person! At the feet of Sadguru Sainath!

Vande Bharat Railway is now at the Shirdi...Sai Nagar Railway Station.

Charlie is getting down from that Railway–happily getting off.

All accompanying people are busy in slogan- making

"Sadguru Sainath Maharaj Ki Jay"

Charlie joins all the crowd – enjoying the mood of one and all.

From there- the "Free Sainath Darshan!" Bus is awaiting for these devotees to board it for Sai Baba's Samadhi. The devotees respectfully make way for our Charlie to board the bus and gets him seated honourably. Bus now leaves for Sai Baba's mausoleum. Pranav doesn't know–whether he is Pranav or is Charlie or entirely someone else or yet another double. Totally confused if this is a matter of rebirth or a product of some wayward genius scientist's experimentation at play. Whether it is simply a God's will demonstrating his strength to make a Superstar out of an ordinary man? He is presently still in that Charlie Getup and having had the Darshan,-comes out of the Core Temple. He then takes a walk to Shirdi Bus Stand that is nearby and there – he gets respectfully seated,- in a Shegaon- bound Bus so as to reach the Sadguru Gajanan Maharaj there-

He realises the respect being given to him by the fellow traveller Devotees and just then the Bus commences its Shegaon Darshan Yatra.

Nanarao's goons also reach Shirdi, based on Media Reports.

Nanarao is deeply upset – very very upset with all the newspaper reports that keep flowing in unabated. His goons now move on to Shirdi as the news of Charlie being in Shirdi has gone viral on the Social Media promptly after his having Sai Baba Darshan. Having seen all those news items,-Nanarao has despatched his goons – But those goons do not get to see Charlie at all as Charlie was already on way to yet another Shrine!

The goons had kept looking out for Charlie around the Temple Periphery while Charlie, in fact had already left for Shegaon. Once again a matter of good luck in favour of our Charlie, dodging the hooligans of Nanarao.

Charlies news ladder was now abuzz with news reports about his escaping from those hooligans and here on the very next day's news that, "***Charlie is Back***!" walked into the News Ladder.

MACHINE VALIDITY– had got expired by two days out of the fifteen days- will Pranav be killed by the Nanarao Mafia?

Will Pranav get caught by these gangsters?

You are now in a dilemma state that there could be some more miracles

What, at all- would you do with one,- who simply does not know –what is in his destiny- In the end, from all practical point of view, it is God alone who is our guide. And we all are–just Tourists on a visit to this Planet.

This one sentence was of the original Charlie Spencer Sir.

As so stated, events now were taking place and Pranav i.e. Charlie travelled for 2 to 3 days all over Maharashtra and visited almost all the prominent shrines one by one.

Yet again – As luck would have it, it is for our Charlie, who now had boarded the train to Mumbai by a mistake.

Train to Mumbai –but Pranav is simply not aware of it.

He has no idea at all about the financial matters. He has not been working with his own intellect which seems to be getting controlled by someone else! Remote control that was controlling his all these –movements, seemed to be being handled by someone unknown. Who was that? It was God himself,- handling this remote control all this time. Pranav Charlie got down just outside a Mumbai Bus stand and he went and sat down under a bridge.

By a coincidence– under that very bridge– Panvel Municipal Corporation was busily running a campaign to catch the psychopaths wandering everywhere. During that campaign, this person,-who is simply not our artist in the dress of Charlie Chaplin but in fact is a psychopath on a wander and so with help of a Charity Organisation,-has been now admitted in the nearest Psychiatric Hospital. This news got viral on the Social Media and in no time – even the Media too got a clue as to what all was happening.

Chapter-20

Journalists in the Media did publish the news of Charlie having been found, but also emphasised on the fact that no one was being given any permission to meet or see Charlie. So, coming up with a novel assignment as a legitimate attempt to overcome this hurdle, the famed reporter Ms. Kartiki convinced the Hospital Management, "That, I would like to make the entire world aware of the nice superb work that your Psychiatric Hospital is doing and has been contributing what kind of noble treatment to better the mental state of patients affected by some physical / psychiatric disease/ infection to brain etc. and in that context, you all should extend me full cooperation. This was how she finally managed to convince the Manager and that resourceful bright young lady instead of opting to go directly to Charlie began taking short interview of all the patients in the hospital.

While moving around in such a way she come across a Character calling himself Junior Laxmikant Berde (A famous Comedy Actor of Marathi Screen) who was sobbing incessantly –muttering something to himself all the time!

Kartiki. The lady Reporter who had become very famous with her frequent news breaks on the 'Soch' Media Channel on TV and had been causing lot many ripples on the Social Media- drawing attention to her efforts at correcting the social reformers going astray, stopped and asked that fellow-"Bhayya, you look to be depressed! That's all! I don't think you are neither mad nor insane or even a mentally disturbed case as being told- you seem to be simply acting like a psychopath ... I somehow think – that you are simply putting on this act of being insane! "

Jr. Berde responded, "Look sister – There are very few people who do genuinely attempt to understand these Mad/Insane category of people. But then what could I even do otherwise? Given the situation I was in.

I did come to Mumbai – to become an Artist,- wasted all my savings and wasted valuable time too and kept on moving door to door,- meeting all Producers, Writers even big names for some good role. See these badly worn -out chappals of mine- they too will show you and also will tell you about how much I must have walked all the time, but all that... was to no avail and I did keep on running all the time aimlessly wasting few good years of my youth.

Bowing to them – All the time...But getting ignored... all the time...

At times to that Director.

At times to the other Producer,

I kept on for months together,

literally begging them for some job,

seeking and begging them for some money to sustain-

and kept on doing all odd jobs, to survive in a way–

Nowhere to my taste- but all for just a Good Role in a Movie -

Such a misery it has been all along the way, Madam!

Experimenting and coping with whatever appeasements that were necessary, that I could think of all tricks that came into my mind, in that period. I had by now,- spent all the money that I had brought when I came here from my village. And if now- I do return to that hometown of mine, people will ask to me surely- "Yes, Laxya! When is your movie getting released? That your super duper big movie...the one you used to tell us all the time?"

Such stinging arrows – they will surely be hitting me with, where at all did I go wrong- I keep on wondering all the time, asking God again and again – crying all alone – the only thing now left to me, so much of a self-inflected misery!

What finally was my fault, that I simply could not become a big Celebrity Artist- so instead,- of getting hurt by such shockful reception in our hometowns- gulping the insults and the bad words from these who were our own people...I just thought,-why not continue staying in a Psychiatric Hospital? Lot many artists like me are here opting to stay here without any hopes of becoming anything at all. And my life – now has become a total waste."

Madam! Do you know that,- someone here thinks of himself as the great Nana Patekar (Celebrity Marathi-Hindi Actor).

Someone is addressed as a duplicate Junior Johny Lever, the Hindi Comedian– Why,-we do have even our own version of yet another Amitabh Bacchan too- giving us his company but then this our world – reduced to a mere dosage of capsules/ tablets twice a day with meals and break-fast and....

And on occasions, even the electric current treatment,

that they give once a week!

That's all there is, as to the remaining part of our ambitious life,- one that we kept dreaming of ! **"That name and fame!"** we keep looking for...

And yet despite all that sorry tale of his own making, he still smiles at Kartiki making her notes.

You don't know what we even went through—like walking on fire? Why is it that you think it was *Sita* alone who did it- we too are doing it all through our lives!

And all this, mind you,- my dear Madam...

Just because of wanting to do something entirely different and far more challenging to achieve some great name and fame and begin to help poor people. Instead of all that, what we really became was just paupers- penniless- idiots and then..as they say.... worthless rats!

It's all your past life *Karmas* revisiting you, perhaps,- as the wise ones do say. Life has been tough, with us madam,- unbearable –un-thought of Listening to all this hurt being poured out, tears swelled in Kartiki's eyes!

And then she signalled her cameraman to cut the scene there itself and said to that Artist,- the duplicate Laxmikant Berde had now started sobbing,- nonstop !

Kartiki responded, "Dada- I will do something and I shall see what can I do about all this – What knowledge can I give you? It is so sad, a sad life!"

While she was moving in –in the other cabin she chanced to see Pranav – in the role and make-up of Charlie lying near the wall and with his legs up along that wall in the closed cabin. He seemed to be sleeping but yet the expressions of

humming to himself, fully immersed in some deep thoughts– is what makes his face twisted in pain. Lips trembling as if he is all the time muttering to himself in that dream sort of thing and so she turns the camera on him to capture that feel of his loneliness mood and find who after all is this guy? What was his real name, background and the secrecy behind all this travel?

Promptly– sensing that camera on him–Charlie shouts out Huryo! and jumps up. Now he is totally out of his self imposed trance – and puts out his hand through the window– trying to shake hands with the Lady Reporter.

Assistant Cameraman swings into action,-following her as usual- takes in that shot..

Charlie (Pranav) pulls out a Rose from his pocket, sits down on the floor and presents the flower to her as if he is proposing! So comic it seemed to all that spontaneity of the unknown Artist.

She sensed even in that mood,-that till now- no one has ever proposed to her and that this guy doing it. He must be really a dead insane guy! And has presented the flower to her without realising her Real Life Status.

And at the same time, she muses! How, is it that this guy dares to propose to me? She becomes wonderstruck and then taking all that footage, she returns to her office with the Asst. Cameraman following her.

In that Sanatorium, that Junior Laxmikant- whom she had met had managed to get her Cell No.- saying if at all in future- if needed to call her,–if he is in trouble sometime and she had then responded favourably to this request of his and so had given him her personal number.

Nanarao's hooligans too- have now come to know the address of the Hospital where Charlie had been admitted- thanks to Media Coverage.

Now- in the upcoming night itself is Pranav/Charlie likely to get murdered? That was the question everyone seemed to wonder about... Kartiki too did also wonder about such an eventuality.

Will Pranav –come in front of the Media?

Can Kartiki come up with any more classic idea to save Pranav?

All this – only.... that Supreme God knows...(Scene cut).

चार्ली चॅप्लिनच्या १२५ व्या जयंतीनिमित्त चार्ली भक्त सोमनाथ यांनी चार्ली चॅप्लिनची वेशभूषा करून मुंबईतील गेटवे ऑफ इंडियाला भेट दिली. यावेळी लोकांचे मनोरंजन करत मतदानाबाबत जनजागृती केली. (छाया : मृगेश बांदिवडेकर)

CHARLIE IS BACK

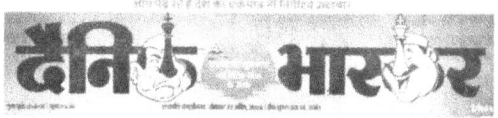

મુંબઈ, બુધવાર તા. ૧૭ એપ્રિલ, ૨૦૨૪

નો ક્રોમેડી પ્લીઝ : ચાર્લી ચેપ્લિનની ૧૩૫મી જન્મજયંતી નિમિત્તે તેમના ચાહક સોમનાથે અદલ ચાર્લી ચેપ્લિનનો જ ગેટ અપ ધારણ કરી ગેટ વે ઓફ ઇન્ડિયા ખાતે જઈ લોકોને આ ચૂંટણીમાં મતદાન અચૂક કરવા સમજાવ્યા હતા. તેમણે તેમને કહ્યું હતું કે આ ચૂંટણી કોઈ હળવાશથી લેવા જેવી બાબત નથી. સૌએ ગંભીરતાપૂર્વક પોતાની ફરજ બજાવી મતદાન કરવું જ જોઈએ.

EVERYMAN ASKS EVERY MAN & WOMAN TO VOTE

Somnath Sawbahvne, a Charlie Chaplin impersonator from Chhatrapati Sambhajinagar, performed for 14 hours at various locations on the icon's 135th birth anniversary to urge voters to be engaged in the polls

INSPIRING THROUGH ART: An artiste from Aurangabad, Somnath Sawbahvne, dressed up as " Charlie Chaplin on the legendary actor's 135th birth anniversary on Tuesday, urges people to " cast votes outside Chhatrapati Shivaji Maharaj terminus. *Ganesh Shirsekar*

Chapter-21

Assistant Dr. Ashish – a greedy kind of a person by way of his nature itself- is taking his usual rounds- in the Psychiatric Hospital– calmly checking the patient, going through the patient's reports... He, at the same time- happens to be a close relative of the owner of the Hospital. He is a Brother-in-Law of the Doctor Saheb and so considers that this Psychiatric Hospital is – in a way – his own father's property – while keeping on attending the routine work, he was in a habit of getting into breaking the usual Hospital Rules –in so far as the Patient's Routine Health Care Records... is concerned.

He, often had this penchant for committing certain breaches of the thoughtfully laid-out Hospital Rules and get fired,- in no uncertain words by his Boss. But then the Boss would still excuse him... for that lapse / oversight – that had been committed- all because this guy happens to be a close relative.

Such is this Boss's kind heartedness- trying to train the junior for some professionalism that had to be cared for,- even in the daily routine.

But in a way from Ashish's point of view– such bosses were, few and in fact –were kind of a severe pain in the Ass as if. Biting one – if one holds him up and, - if one does leaves it undisturbed / overlooked, it would simply run off- (being the one related to that supreme), Such kind of a man is this Boss Mindset! That was the summation he had reached by now!

But then this Supreme Boss- DN Sir- as addressed by all, had, in fact, earned all his riches, by just honest ways. He always displayed this noble nature of his and was running and administering the Hospital in a genuine 'Service-Mode!.' For benefitting the poor-helpless patients- who had nowhere to go nor did have anyone to care about them. His,- this very simple nature– slightly emotionally sensitive one as a temperament –was the prime reason for opting to invest all his this hard-earned and well-saved riches- made him– set up this well –equipped hospital extending a 24X7 care- for the benefit of the less-blessed–dependant category of people–needing that Motherly Care,- something he

knew,- he could definitely handle better than others.

But then –some people-working in such institutions – do have that desire to earn a bit more- extra income in addition to what was being paid as their true worth. All this out of greed– thereby achieving their own selfish interests in one or other ways while posing as selfless noble servers of Humanity. Dr. Ashish was just one of this kind.... always seeking more and more! He exercised caution– so that the Dr. DN– would go on delegating him more and more of authority in maintaining the regular decorum of the Hospital to the desired levels so that Hospital License wouldn't get tarnished. Dr. Ashish was sure that, the Doctor would never tolerate any such negligent behavioural lapses while on duty. Such a lapse would obviously be leading to that Supremo making him to open his third eye... that might even lead to getting thrown off from hospital in a royal kick off leading to dismissal.

Doctor Shiv Har Trinetre !

MBBS- A Master Psychiatrist!

That is the visiting card used by the Supreme Boss,-whom he called the Supremo– in private!

Since he had chosen to be on leave- availing it after a long time- this Assistant had got an opportunity to look after the entire routine work of the Hospital and ensure that routine Healthcare Parameters are being properly taken care of and attended to. So he,-Dr. Ashish stood elevated as the Hospital Head during the time of Boss's vacation.

While the routine was getting attended to – this Assistant heard the Hospital phone ringing...

Patients around him- have dozed off to sleep- in their own special rooms-   That would remind one... of the prison rooms- little bit better version– but still reminding one of that prison atmosphere.

And as such – he, without giving any thought as to who would be on line- he did pick up that phone directly –

That phone call- was by none other than our own Dear Nanarao- the famed film Producer / Director.

Dr. Ashish began to speak on the phone...non –stop...

"Hi! The Producer Director Nanarao Sir-in person!

Sir, can you tell me what all is going on?

"Do tell me in brief as to what exactly are you upto?

How many CRs - you want us to keep on correcting / changing /modifying to suit your needs? Needs that are never –ending."

Now–We– In fact have got six –six licenses in our hands already and I really wonder if the office bearers of that institution that issue licenses- they seem to me to be perfect idiots.I don't think they do understand the gravity part of their being such in-charges. They do not seem to really understand at all what exactly their job is about?

And on the other side...

Take a look at our Boss!

He-my own relative –an elderly man-

Should have happily retired by now-

He is of that type of people-who just can't think of retiring from active life!

They, that kind of people who cherish tasting the ghee/ butter – on either side –even if brought in a ready to eat mode.

And not just that- they don't even let

anyone else have any such pleasure too!

Won't let anyone have even a slight bit more of butter.

How one wishes to taste that butter-and

He-ever watching would promptly notice it-

He will come up with a right way to hold

The one who attempted it-

That's because he- himself perhaps knows– how to bend his fingers– dip them into that ghee and chew it all by himself.

Isn't that so – my dear Saheb? (Finally his this outburst stops).

Nanarao: Hey! you Ashish!- don't go on cracking jokes like whenever you feel like – Someone who may be listening from nearby – someone standing beside you- will start becoming jealous of you- and create more problems for you. Let me tell you first what I am calling about.

I was told that- in your Hospital – you have got hold of a man- a mad man – if you want me to say so- that mad fellow – was loitering around the roads in Mulund sector- wearing a complete make-up of Charlie Chaplin- that legendary Comedy Actor! Now– we need him, back here at the studio just quickly – And hey! Listen to this –no one should get any clue about what I am saying /telling you.

Ashish: Wow! What in the world, you are telling me Bro!

You've got your hand –behind this also – this Charlie business?

Oh! We have been all the time attending to your whims!

God alone knows how many such cases – missing identities may keep on coming up,-telling us- that they are so and so and are now here forever! Having sold all their agricultural lands / holdings– they attempted to become someone else- Something much more tempting– become mad at the way they get mistreated here in the jungles of humans like you,- in that Film City.

Then there are those hooligans- who keep on being on lookout for such idiots. You then to go on to tempt them – those poor souls- that they themselves are gifted human beings,-moving in wrong places promising them that they too could become like yesteryear Superstars – if they just abide by your instructions. We will make you Einstein / Pluto/ Ceaser and now this time, the turn of Charlie Chaplin, has come up.

Nanarao: Ashish– that is enough for now. Now you better listen to me carefully. This Chaplin story might turn out to be quite dangerous- you better tell that Actor that he is un-wellcome and he is to leave the hospital immediately and tell all others who might want to know about his whereabouts. Now you better simply put out that he simply ran away and we have no idea –where he might have gone. Leave all this at that point and I shall take over from that point itself.

Ashish : No ! No! Nanarao – now nothing like that can be done or can be so handled.

Nanarao: Look here Ashish, For God's sake, let us stop this mind-game of chess immediately. If I even move a few pieces here and there, you can be sure that you won't be able to avoid a check mate situation in no time at all. I'll be able to tell all –whose black money is being recycled again and again as white money- by running your that mental hospital-Whose black money- all this is? It belongs to which organisation. That under the guise of CSR funding – your boss – has set up this racket of Black Money Conversion. You guys get all that done up to convert all that black money into white money and portray a Nobility picture of how unselfish you all are. I do wish to tell you this – I do have a complete file on you guys- have even the minor details also, so you better stop all this nonsensical talk and get this work done promptly. We have only this one night in our hands. Matter is awfully serious, don't take anything of this lightly. We shall all get destroyed if we don't handle this crisis promptly, and cautiously.

Ashish: Oh! that all is right sir- If you checkmate me or I checkmate you – either way it will lead to incurring losses for both of us- and everyone associated. But then what can now be done? Media has managed to set up a campaign of interviewing all the patients that are here. Charlie has also been interviewed as a part of that program. We will have to produce him in a Court of Law tomorrow morning itself to check if he really is crazy psychopath – or just an Actor – He is in fact, quite active when he is in that actor mode and a total nobody when he isn't aware of what's being asked- Lives totally in an Acting mode and is very active. Media Reporters- are having a field day for such unbelievable News. You better take care- I'll see what can be done on my side.

Let us leave playing each others, this mind-game of chess and let us now play a game of how to make more business yet out of this all.

Nanarao: I shall send you the scanner codes of five or six organisations as I will have a problem now-leaving this situation as it is. You now tell your friend circle / families to quickly arrange to send at least Rs. 50 Lakhs as a Gift / Donation and once I receive those 50 Lakh here, I shall be able to announce that the said person has committed suicide. So you get on to do all this work and I for myself,- will begin my share of the work before us. Forget this game of chess- Let's play our Business Card as best as we can – even under these conditions.

Chapter-22

By a sheer coincidence it was in just last three – four days- there had been that Maha Shivratri festival and Pranav had appeared at all the major shrines in Maharashtra and had taken a Darshan of this Supreme Deity. He was not bound by any of the so called social restrictions. There was total freedom that would welcome him. He had been to Haji Masjid as well. Even went into a temple and a church also– spreading a feel of pure pleasure- happiness –everywhere as a man who had gone ahead in creation of bliss and even spread it personally this bliss within oneself. Everywhere he chose to go and bow before the Deities there, with his fans applauding his activities.

And now what exactly had been going in the real life of such an Artist?

And by yet another coincidence– today was what they call as "बडीरात" (Badi - Raat) meaning night from morning itself Ramazan would commence.

And just one part- a degree only... of this Universe was Pranav himself.

And the other degree we all each one of us. What is likely to happen, this very thought was accentuating our heart beats.

Never before such a silence.... total silence,-was ever felt in that Psychiatric Hospital! All the patients were in their own rooms and along with them the eternally humming sound of mosquitoes.

Pranav was in his own room – all alone.

He simply has no worries at all

Nor was he under any tension too!

In pure joy- he was now lost...as he was now in his own... Acting Mode!

Hey! You tell me- So innocent and ignorant this character is. Death is standing on his head literally.

Has no ideas as to where his parents are now nor knows where he hails from which place,- and no one knows what all is going to happen to you or what all will be happening to you?

And just then... there itself

Junior Laxya! Having a severe headache ...

In his own room-

With his head clasped tightly between the two pillows nearby and sobbing all the time- incessantly.

That junior Laxya! Muttered to himself!

"Oh! My God! Never heard of anything like this!

What a story - Never heard / Never saw such a thing,

And if – I cannot help him to get out from here before those rascals come here ,- then with what face will I be coming to you,

Whenever my own life ends!

Give me a chance to become a Hero in the movies
Give me that one opportunity to me-
Was all that I used to beg you and
I used to say keep saying to you all the time
But then....
What at all you have now brought before me.
Tell me what can I do about it –
How at all, I can help this Charlie trapped in that neighbouring cabin.
I cannot believe those gangsters at all-
He perhaps – has only few more hours to live on!
One cannot trust those hooligans.
When at all will they suddenly reach here and attack the poor fellow!
What will they be doing?
God- You are my only *Maula*,
I totally trust in you and your fair play.
If there's someway out of all this then-
Do tell me – Enlighten me as to that-
My own parameter – Tell me what am I to do?"

The look on his face-
Surfacing around him a bit of an Aura-
Seems to have suggested ...
Now something to him-
He promptly gets up now and shakes all his clothes...
In those clothes – that phone number- of that Lady who had visited,
It says it is the number of Media Reporters.
A Smile now on Laxmikant's face!

Wide grin ... at that break!
He takes a beautiful, a fond kiss of that number
As if,- it now the only ray of light
Emanating out of all that darkness –
crowding that dear friend of his.
(Scene cut at this step).

✦ ········ ✦

Chapter-23

In the Media House Office of
"THE SOCH CHANNEL!"
Representatives – and Members of Staff
Keep on moving all the time
And at the Reception counter
One young lady is laughing –
while listening to someone else's call.
Just then Kartiki- the famous Lady Reporter comes in.

Kartiki- (To the Receptionist busy listening to someone else's pone)

Ha! Ha! Ha! Do keep on listening to someone else's telephone calls –

Never do anything yourself and just by listening to what other people are doing and do, is it not what you are always upto. I have now found that epicentre of Rumour–creation,- from where all kinds of rumours spread from. Ha! Ha! Ha! I have found that focal point I must say. I will tell all.. this great discovery of how to verify the rumours.. by eavesdropping! Ha! Ha! Ha!

All those odd things that keep on happening in the office and the database of all people as to, 'who is with whom' and 'where they are going to'- all that one can get to know from this focal point itself!

Receptionist : Hey Kartya- There's nothing like that! Am just doing a little bit of my own detective work sitting from here itself. Whenever the boss calls you in,-show him all that Psychiatric Hospital Visit Data- you have brought and I am quite sure you are bound to get promoted.

Kartiki- (Wonderstruck and in a happy mood goes towards that Cabin. There the News Head Executive and the very owner of Channel are seated. Ravi Kisan Sir! Sitting in his cabin – he was talking with someone on phone about a mater far important and she enters the Cabin.)

Ravi Sir:(Says to the other man on phone) I will call you up again shortly. Turning towards Kartiki- he said, "Come! Come! Kartiki Madam! What report you have for us now? About that Psychiatry Hospital,- you visited today?"

Kartiki: Oh! Sir, The Report about that Psychiatric Hospital is just routine. But the doubt that I have is that something else is going on over there. I have a gut feel that there seems to be a misuse of what we call as CSR funding, by some of the Corporate Organisations, perhaps in collusion with the Hospital Management.

But this time, a psychiatric got admitted in the Hospital by Panvel Corporation Authorities. That guy was moving around the streets and of all the things he was doing the role of Charlie Chaplin live and entertaining the traffic all the time, thereby creating problems. The news that we been showing and the other News Reports that herald "**Charlie is**

Back!" that same person – the original Charlie etc. now is said to be not an actor but in fact is just a psychiatric case, perhaps a psychopath,-that is now being investigated. At that Hospital, itself, they have been instructed to produce him tomorrow – in the Court of Law and it is being said that he will, now on,- be staying in that hospital on a permanent basis – That kind of future planning is being talked about and he simply doesn't even have any I.D. that is required nor does anyone knows from where he actually comes from.

Ravi Kisan: Well, Kartiki- a nice job- Now listen to me.

Just load all that footage– that you have brought from there in to my pen drive and delete all the data– that's with you.

We are enhancing your post level. You will now on... be designated as a District Chief Editor. Along with the promotion you are being given an increment as well. You are very much now on way to become a District Level Admin as well. Take a paid vacation for four days, have a good rest from today onwards itself, preparing for the added responsibility coming your way. On the fifth day, I shall tell you where to go and yes,-in meantime do delete all other irrelevant data that's with you. For your information, it was a decision reached in our Media Association that no more publicity is to be given to this news–otherwise... what might happen could be,- any other normal human-being might also begin to parade around as yet another Charlie– specially like this Character prone to Psychiatric Ailments – One might get into yet another Charlie Make-up and we might keep on harping once again in the same way. There has to be a well laid-out limit for all such things in future.

"Charlie is Back!!!"

We don't want 'Gossip' to get increased beyond tolerable limits.

We have a target of ensuring that, our Channel does go on recording the progress in this matter and the pay packet that you will be now on receiving will merit a careful attention by you.

Come on,- do get all that data deleted from you mobile–but before that you safely deposit all that you've got till now,- into my pendrive by tonight.

Kartiki: Sir, if it all is to be deleted – why at all should be loaded into your or anybody's pendrive, for that matter?

Ravi Kisan: I said so- Isn't it? Your promotion is likely to happen right now- Listen – who spent how many days and where exactly,-all such reports- I do need to have as Office Records.

Kartiki:(smiles) Having just a little fun, sir!

Wow my promotion and a four day paid vacation too!

What a lucky stroke all this!

How come the Deities have given me all these unexpected boons, I wonder!

Saying and smiling at the same time, here she does take out her pendrive from her laptop- hands it over to Kisan sir and comes out of the cabin with her laptop.

Now in a totally happy mood- she goes to the reception table and says to her friend, "Hey –aren't you still over with your day? Come along I am feeling like throwing party for you as I am in a happy mood. Let us party together."

Receptionist – No Yaar! I have to play this role as a receptionist in the night hours, and today being '*BadiRaat*!' Salimbhayya may not come for night duty. His Rozas will beginning from tomorrow itself and so for the night today. I have been told to do overtime.

So tonight I will be all alone at the reception in the office itself. But I am available on phone.

Kartiki: (With a smile)

Then shall I bring something to have a party, right here itself!

No Yaar! Don't worry! I know about your addiction to listening to calls of people is more of a gimmick to anticipate any danger or likely disturbance. That 'Coding' aspect you have learnt is also something I do know- But you are misusing all that knowledge at wrong places – is the doubt... that I am worried about.

Receptionist: Why? My dear lady! I shall stop telling you stories related to you- That's all I will say to you for now. Not upstairs – but now in the upper cadre – role – duly promoted..and a promotion,- so well deserved one!

Kartiki: I shall avail that four days vacation and it will be only later on, we shall just meet because I am promoted and then meet you at the send off.

I shall be bidding a goodbye to this office then.

Receptionist: Kisanrao gave you a four day vacation and promotion as well. But yet there is a question mark on your face?

Kartiki too had begun to realise this question mark on her own face- something seemed to have gone wrong – some salt – she thought could be in that glass full of milk. That was what the thought now in her mind.

But the four day paid leave made her keep on thinking of something? Is Kartiki going to be shocked by some untold aspect,-was what now on her mind. All this only that God-Super Planner Paramatma alone knows ...

✦ ········ ✦

Chapter-24

To sit cozily in an embrace of her own 'ocean- father', to sit calmly at the Marine Drive-Seashores and for the sole purpose for this new muse that had stuck in her mind. For this muse,- that of deleting all the data in her laptop- and the four day paid leave a matter of suspicion! That possibility did make her introvert.

Parking her car by the side of the road,-Directing both her legs towards the wall on seashore. Lighting up a cigar in her mouth- she now relaxed a bit. She did puff once or twice the cigar,-in a mood, in fact now in a trance of her own... and while in that mood- she got the files pertaining to that Psychiatry Hospital visit on her laptop. Deleted a few – and while yet deleting- that Charlie...Charlie's totally ignorant- innocent face came up and she recollected a scene that had been enacted there! That funny act of his proposing to her!

That momentary relief act that had livened her up. That game,-the fun of it (brought along a smile as well) now all the time on her mind- mind itself getting engrossed in that small memorable incident.

She was now seeing THAT VIDEO alive in her mind as well. The way in which,- he had got down to the floor in front of her... holding out to her a fresh rose- so tender a flower and his,- this so unexpected an attempt on his part to propose. But then she realised...

She just couldn't got that video deleted from her mind. Why–what happened – She was now lost in her own muse!

Why am I not able to delete this video?

Why is it that I, too, do not feel like – deleting that video...? She kept on wondering!

Deleting not in the laptop nor in my mind as well. So she kept on wondering.

A slowed down mind..that one-

the Pranav guy decidedly a retarded one.

A Psychiatrist patient – A psychopath– a better term. He is giving me a rose 'of all the things' and me,-a young attractive girl– how come this guy seeming so heavy to me- to carry him in my mind-

She kept on, seeing that video again and again.

All other data did get deleted.

But this video –

Why is it that I too am now,-

Not feeling like deleting it?

That boyish look on his face.. And she sensed that...

Someone sat beside her..

He too affected by that wonderful shot

Watching that very video – tears came into his eyes as well.

But this happens to be

Mumbai – A metropolis

Here no one speaks to anyone!

Each one lives as per his free wish-

Here- there happens to be no restriction whatsoever.

One should live in our own style, that is the convention....

That in fact is the Mumbai Version of a lifestyle adopted by all those residing here. With no time for humaneness; running around all the time-in their own mad rush of,- trying to make both ends meet.

Now that someone...

One who had sat beside her.

Taking in all that scenario he had been watching intently..

That gentleman (Dr.Shiv Har Trinetre) said to her...

'Madam Kartiki- Did you recognise me?'

"Oh! My dear Sir! How come you are here?"

Dr.Shiv Har Trinetre then commented...

"This Mumbai itself is my mother and also my father! "

I was born in a nearby village and...

As I too was just an unwanted child of someone....

Someone had dumped me there

And when I grew up..

Because I had become bit aware,

Of all that was going around

I came to know then itself....

That those who had dumped me there

Were in fact– they too were our own people!

But now all that- how at all would it matter?

For one,- who doesn't have anyone

To take his care for himself only.

There is this *Mumbadevi* Mother and *Siddhivinayak*

Taking care of me as my Dad!

And *Haji Ali* playing role of a Brother!

And all the Gods- Goddesses- my relatives in this Mumbai?

He then wipes out the corner of his eyelids now wet with tears.

Let that be so –

Let's leave that matter.

We will talk about all that after sometime-

How come – you got this Charlie's video, where at all and do tell me –

How come,- you seem to be so restlessly sitting here like me?

Kartiki: Oh! No! Nothing to worry about – but Sir, I had been to your Psychiatric Hospital today. I was told that you are on a 4 day holiday – that was what your Assistant there... told me but did give me permission to shoot these pictures. To make it a Big News about the noble work, you all are doing there- I did take a Cameraman alongwith me and did some Video shooting too. I picked up some interesting and heart ripping footages of the agonies suffered by some of your psychopath patients! It is in that footage I got this shot- This psychopath named Charlie has come there –

It was Police Authorities – who have got him admitted there after the Panvel Corporation Staff had found him– sitting under a Road Bridge.

Dr.Shiv Har Trinetre: I see, but Madam– do you have any idea why at all I had taken this 4 day holiday?

You see – it was this very Charlie– who had brought out my grandson, son of my daughter,-out from a severe depression mode that he was in and a friend of mine- whose children had become totally mobile addicts– they too had now got out of that severe depression mode. All those people had thought that it was myself– who had sent this Charlie as a surprise pleasure to cheer up all these depressed kids- trying to keep them away from this mobile addiction and so had organised that picnic for that school.

So many serious cases of mobile addiction among these new generation kids is a matter of great concern.

And some of them, have got into a severe addiction for these mobiles. They simply cannot stay without them.

The teacher,- too said, "That my own child too is admitted for a retrieval from this severe mobile addiction that you saw. Both myself and my wife used to be very busy in earning money all the time– to maintain the household and ensure better days for the kids. We had a housemaid hired to look after our son and she- when kids used to be with her would give each one of them a mobile to play with. She gave them these mobiles to keep them engaged and what's more she too would keep on playing her own mobile for hours together.

Those people, who had provided me that house-maid had considerable number of such mobile addict cases and lot many parents had approached them for supplying such house-maids to keep the kids under safe care.

An horrible habitat – leading to sever addiction and that too right from that tender age!

So horrible – Do you know- just for sake of having mobiles with them all the time- these kids go to the extent of even murdering their own parents-getting so awfully habituated with mobile. They just can't live without them.

So it was with such kind of children that Charlie met them in a forest and he made them pass their time with him. So they all thought that, it was myself who had sent Charlie there to divert the kids from mobiles to much more lively things, and so they urgently put out a call for me.

And then I was busy and tied up- attending to kids, and trying to search out this Charlie fellow everywhere and literally I too did get exhausted. Tired by that run-around, they are jumping to the conclusion that, he is a psychopath but it was this psychopath– who cured all those children – pulling them out of that ghastly depression mode and that too by just a one day exhibition of his brain-wave about spreading pleasure everywhere he goes. Hey! Come along! We got to get back to our own Hospital. Call it Ashram if you too like it. We got to meet this guy!

And..

In Kartiki's inner mind...

A flame- of one sided love had sparked up.

It got converted into a speech and– and that spark ignited flared up in no time so without deleting that video she happily took a screenshot of it and said –"yes sir, let's move!".This is what she said to Dr.Shiv Har Trenetre.

Since she had not been seeing the phone that had begun ringing again and again – she now looked at it and said, "Sir just a minute! Someone seems to have been calling me up for a long time- but I didn't pick it up- let me take that call."

Kartiki picks up the phone- "Hello! Who is this?"

Junior Laxmikant : Oh! My dear Taisaheb, I have been ringing you for since so long a time. Too tough getting you on line- It is now that I am getting a chance to speak to you.

Subject is damn serious. Charlie– the Actor now,- is still here-

In the cabin that's beside mine- I am reasonably sure that in just a short while- some hooligans/ gundas- are likely to come and might hurt the fellow in my neighbouring cabin, who has been acting in that Character Role of Charlie Chaplin ! I am 100% sure of their these mal-intentions - All would be vagabonds, unbothered about law etc. You are a famous reporter of the Media and so I decided to call you up, as you had given me your personal number...

Do something about it Madam- May be this poor guy might even lose his life. As the phone was still on,-with its speaker on...Laxya's voice did reach Dr.Shiv Har Sir and he promptly recognized that voice. He said, "Hey! Kartiki- This voice is of a patient in our own Psychiatry Hospital!" Come, quick let's go – We got to do something about all this –once for all!

What all is happening?

Call from Kartiki's Office

Receptionist: Kartiki – better take care of yourself – Do not meet anyone or any stranger for that matter. Some people are likely to keep following you. Don't go to your home. Go to some unknown place. I sense some kind of trouble coming your way – Take care!

Kartiki- responds: Hey! Shweta! What happened?

Shweta : Ever since sir took that footage from you about your Hospital visit- he has been receiving calls from various phone numbers and Sir too has been making all kinds of odd commitments to the calling parties. I thought the matter is far more serious – so I thought of cautioning you up- and alert you.

Fright and sweat were now being clearly seen on Kartiki's face. Just then Sir said to her, "Don't get afraid, Kartiki- We are both together in this. I, am with you here. Do not get afraid." He called up his Hospital. Dr. Ashish promptly picked up the phone.

Dr.Ashish: Hey! My dear Brother-in-law, no trace of yours! My sister was telling me you have gone to your town at your son's Hospital. How is his health?

Dr Shiv Har Trinetre: Hello- Ashish! "I was too busy. What all is going on in our Ashram. Is everything all right?"

Just then Dr.Trinetre sees Kartiki- signalling him not to say anything – he understands it and he, now clearly,-just to divert Ashish's mind – said 'I have came towards this Congress Bhavan Sector!'

Ashish: Wow! You are quite a Chupa Rustum! Ya!

Dr.Trinetre: No! No! Nothing like it- Some other work made me go there.

Ashish (in a naughty mood):Something like saying...I am sitting in a bar and have ordered a *Masala Milk* for myself. Let that be! No problem at all on this side- Everything normal. Patients came and have gone. Routine work is going on as usual. Do not take any tension whatsoever. If you don't feel like coming tomorrow as well,- don't worry. I will take care as usual –

Got to attend the routine. The way it keeps unfolding...

Both the Doctor and Kartiki now have a 100% doubt. Their vehicle speedily moves towards the Ashram. Kartiki is ringing up someone. To create confusion amongst those following her, Kartiki has left her own vehicle at Marine Drive,-itself and it is in the Doctor's vehicle that they both have been sitting and having thought of something altogether afresh.

Are Kartiki and Dr. Shiv Har Trinetre together as one team?

Will Kartiki's considered one way affair will now become a two-way traffic. Would Kartiki succeed in her this attempt to ensure that Pranav Charlie's life remains safe? Oh! That Mumbai Night life! And what to say of it? was now the thought that had struck Dr.Ashish!

✦ ········ ✦

Chapter-25

One bereft man
No recognition –
Has no identity – No known connections
No background whatsoever!
What could be the relationship of these two persons with our Pranav- Charlie?
That one- a relationship of just humanness!
Or something coming from their last birth.
How at all can we know about it?
We, all on this planet and in this Universe of ours;
Humans inhabiting this planet earth -
Just ordinary human beings.
Not craving for money
But in a relationship
Shared as fellow human beings.
Those who did so much till now...
And finally became more of a History to all ?
Every individual who thus became a part of History
Not attempting to do anything for oneself.

But having done a lot for others around.
Such an individual this one.....
Whether a woman or a man
Or some animal or even just a birdie!
He.. the one who lives for only himself
Does live here.. for just a while..
But that one who lives for others
In a selfless mode of living,-
Just for sake of others,
It is that person who creates History
And because the History- getting so personified

This is what goes on happening ..
Selfless living – living only for others.
That itself has been History for others to emulate!

In much the same way,
Because these fellow have been attempting all along..
Something – a bit speedily-putting
All their hearts into those efforts.
This attempt of theirs,-we don't even understand.
But one thing is sure that...
For saving the life of a pure soul –
Of an ignorant innocent one..
They keep on attempting...
To the best of their wits,
knowledge and what's more –
Risking their own lives in return!
All this mechanism- the social movements –
Aren't very easy things to decipher...

To get properly understood..
Wouldn't be that easy at all !
The way it does,- sounds so superficially!
Money! It's money alone that matters against money!
That aspect – itself has assumed so big a proportion these days....
All for just Fame, Name and Wealth –
They seem to be just everything that is worthwhile and worthy of attention.

We never seem to even think about
The precious power of Nature –
So visible around us- all the time –
Those that are available in abundance
Nature and Grains etc. so vital for living!
We don't seem to even think for a moment
About these produce of nature
That makes life lovable and liveable as well !
Before we really came here on this Earth
Someone did find
A way of producing grains for us.
Before we had even got born.
Someone did create a food chain on this earth,
Sufficient enough to let humans survive
Help animals, birds and humans to sustain –
We yet thanklessly - as thought forget all these boons
And go on boasting all the time...
What did I do? What all I did? What all shall I be doing all the time?
It is in this introspectiveness

Within oneself that we go on fighting all along
Fight on and on and finally die...someday
When Death visits us in His last call!

We did come here with totally empty hands...
And we shall also be leaving with the same empty hands.

Kartiki (Speaks out): Sir- on the Social Media-

Charlie is Back# This *Hashtag* /trend has been going on and on! All the video shots of his visiting those holy shrines have, all gone viral.

Soon those, all people, who would wish to see Charlie- shall be creating quite a crowd in our suburb around our Psychiatrist Hospital and it shall be because of the presence of this huge crowd– that we shall be saving his life. That crowd will ensure that the so called psychopath is safely delivered to your custody. How he has got saved till now that too has been just because of this massive crowd or public in response to the publicity that man got on the Social Media! Now it has dawned on all these people who are concerned.... that when he is mixed up amid that crowd,- no one can do any harm to him and... well... he too will be far more happier to be among those common citizens.

Come on! let us reach that Psychiatry Hospital of ours as fast as we can!

Dr.Shiv Har Trentre: Ok Kartiki, will we be staying on this planet tomorrow? I don't seem to think we will but, by then,-we would have done a big work. Because of which an innocent-ignorant pure soul will be getting saved and while departing from this world, I will be able to close my eyes and happily end my living here -without sensing any weight or feeling any moral burden,-whatsoever on my mind in that last moment- prior to that ultimate exit of mine.

I have thought about what I shall now be doing as to that Psychiatry Hospital and that's why I am accepting the responsibility of this his guardianship and move to go into that Court- where, I am sure they will all attempt to get him declared as a man with no identity and so under the guise of a "Treatment" clause,- might as well try to wipe out his very existence and a great history that is being written merely on the basis of strength of money power and all this,- just out of personal selfishness, and on the basis of the strength of dictatorship of vested interests being exercised all along. We all know that, lot many saints and priests have been forced into an oblivion– by issuing statements like – Oh! He took 'Samadhi' or like 'simply has passed away'!

Today- in this digital age such fallacies being fed to the life histories of such noble souls,-more because everything is just a click away-

So there really is no need for us to go there,-right now. Now listen to this from me, Kartiki- An Affidavit of my this Guardianship Intention has already been submitted by me online. So we will get ourselves...an online guardianship of our Charlie temporarily,- until you go to the Psychiatric Hospital.

I am taking up this guardianship of him as his elder brother. And as it is,- every citizen of India is already either my brother or a sister- leaving apart just one...!

Kartiki:- What do you mean by that-

"Leaving apart from just one! "

What are you precisely talking of?

Dr.Shiv Har Trinetre: Hey! I was just trying to crack a joke.

Now at this moment – we shall live this movement...in pure joy.

"Leaving Apart One!" Oh! That you see, if I am to call all of them as my brothers and sisters,- then who would be my wife. How do you expect me to call my wife as a sister?

So leaving my wife –apart

All others are very much my own brothers and sisters.

Ha! Ha! Ha!

Chapter - 26

Of lives that unfold themselves!

Dr. Shiv Har Trinetre now glanced at his watch. He then said to Kartiki-

"Look here- my dear! It is already, 3 a.m. Too late, now to reach our homes and we are both in this happy mood. Happy that, - now no damage will reach our – Charlie.

And as it is your car- It is still there on that Marine Drive Seashore, where we both had left it.

We shall drive to that point slowly– looking at the Glamorous Night Life of Mumbai- showering all its glory all along the route.

So glamorously done up Bars & Restaurants. Costly but with those lovely damsels dancing there for the entertainment of people,-who get drawn by the tremendous lighting that is on their structures and do walk-in and launder easy money they have earned.

As it is I am used to early mornings and fortunately a dashing young mind like yours is with me now,- sharing my thoughts- as to a meaningful life. So why not extend our this companionship, is the thought now on my mind. We will be getting there on that seashore, the same spot where we were before and we shall sit there and chat again on the other topics of our common interest. And we then take that early morning walk the one,- that I cherish a lot..What do you think of this suggestion of mine, my dear Kartiki? Of this my suggestion of sharing few more creative thoughts, while walking along.

It isn't always you do have a companion who is open to all such ideas and thoughts but you fortunately,-have a gifted mind,- something that I genuinely admire.

That caring habitat of yours – and being so concerned about the healing of these wounds suffered by those who are in fact, total strangers and yet you want to come up with some sensible relief..even for them. And preciously that also is my approach behind running this Psychiatric Care Hospital. It ain't just some Neurologic Dump Yard where you can Dump Living Corpses. That is my message at this juncture to all those who matter. Am not concerned about who those people are or from where these patients come. To me they are just my patients needing my care.

I am not concerned for things like, they belong to what caste- what community, what religion or for that matter wherefrom these patients hail from. All I know is that they need that personal care, the one that,– I can provide for them! That they are patients, my dear...and that too for no personal fault of theirs, and the situation about being unable to even grasp what had really happened to them.

Living .. just like that

Nothing on mind to aspire for..

Day or night it simply doesn't matter to them at all, -
Such their condition!
(Takes a pause for a while only)
You know Kartiki!
I often have been sitting there– in the Hospital
Gloomily looking at those patients
Locked in their this shelter and....
Those cabins somehow resembling the prison cells-
Eating whatever is being given,-sipping whatever distributed....
For just the sake of it!
Lifeless eyes! Staring into nothing! Brooding all alone!
Poor Souls!...All these poor people,-called as less-blessed.
They.. they my dear Kartiki,
Let me tell you something about them..
Do you know who they are?
They.. they are just living corpses, my dear!
Can't let them die,- uncared for!
And when they do finally die... in a legally correct interpretation
And get packed into some lousy bag by the support staff...
Can lay their hands upon at that time and are ...
Shifted to the Crematorium or Coffin Chambers...
And the authorised signatory....
Filing an affidavit as to no successors...
And issuing a Death Certificate on behalf of the Hospital...
Washing our hands of our responsibility...
To yet another soul that has gone by!
(They get to sit at same place where they had met earlier)

Life! So much of misery around
Disability of mind... the mind itself a mystery in its own way
Totally disabled / retarded!
Just Dumb like....such these souls
Gulping food and tablets given by the support staff
Under Medical Supervision.
Unaware of Death's continuous watch!
I, too, at times do drink and ponder....
Even Mr. Death must have got ....
Pained by all this misery around!
Must have wiped tears in his eyes as well..
A flame getting off... Shutting off the Light Within..
Dreams.. never dreamt before...
Remain shattered,-Identities of these dead ones.
Sold to some greedy gangsters minting money,-
By gross misuse of those identities
Burial of justice– being the name of that act-
Is all that I say of it at times.
That alone a reason for this Hospital Care, my dear Kartiki.
But now am still under a shock, trying to recover...
Am I helping them or am I punishing them ,
Tell me that my dear friend!
Look at that guy Charlie –
A different perspective
Coming all the way
From nowhere- all a matter of....'Lost Memories'
No past to reflect and nor any desire for any great future
Yet memories of those roles lived by himself...

Playing a character that had caught his imagination....
That of the little tramp im-memorable role.
Spreading Laughter all around.
And while I was all this...
An incessant cry... deep inside me...
For the lost identity and
The accompanying Memory loss..
Is far more hurting one ...
Than even those fearful
Heartbreaks we speak about
What to say of Heart failures
Life never beat within these robotic genes of the corpses
Just breathing and yet dragging themselves
To that morrow, the tomorrow they need-
One that never is dawning..
Same ambulance of Panvel Municipal Corporation
Will be carrying them back to Crematorium,
The one that has been dumping such guys
(Having no identities) on us— For our Care and ...
We trying our utmost, unconcerned about all this but yet....
Availing Grants / Donations/ Aid by the like minded patrons.
Building Hospitals with all essential amenities
/ Seeking Praise and the Cheap Publicity that comes with it
Building an Image of Nobleness...
And the ever-elusive mode of living
Camouflaged under that selfishness.
(While standing up and starting their morning walk together)

Can't pity their plight,- or those helpless souls...
They are the ones who think about their miseries and...
Say it's all the past Karmas- knocking on their door the Past Life Guilts - coming back to them
As though on a revisit,-
This time on a revenge mission,-
Guilts they don't even recollect in this atmosphere.

Kartiki, I myself too a dumped child
Dumped near the village Panchayat Seat..
Picked up by some women
Thrown there by some other woman
Background unknown..
So to me.. all those 'Mentals' are....
My own real cousins– sort of
Try to take,- as much care
Or am I punishing them all the more
Making them live more and more
Happiness – they seek – console they seek
Love they seek –
Was what the
Churches, Masjids, Temples said...
Do they even know what is happiness?
I do ask....
Chief Admin of the Hospital
"Oh! Sure! That is my job profile."
I keep seeing the plight of these poor souls
Staying on in a kind of a slightly better,-
But nevertheless a dump yard!

We try making them smile at the wounds suffered by them
CARE- A MATERNAL TOUCH is what we extend..
Kind hearted Doctors...
Seeking to do their own little bit of ...
Virtuosity could be a factor- in their mind
But all said..
All this a punishment for genuine
well-wishers of mankind...
The sight of these souls...
Limping on ... and on...
Days- Months –Years Rolling by –
Few smiles coming their way-
People watching them as exhibits.... during their visits
Is what I sometimes feel..of those scenes...
Getting pained deep within
I try to cheer them up and
Go back to my own bed..
After the tiresome day is over.
And then in the Midnight hours –
When I keep thinking on and on....
And sensing an 'Helplessness' engulfing me...
As the lights are put off in the general ward..
Chief Admin wishing all a Good Night!
And going to sleep with tears in eyes.
Head dug deeply between two pillows
To deter a severe headache...
A blanket now pushed all over the body ..
Day... drawing to an end.

All acts till now,
And we with eyes wide open all thru the night
Seeking Blessing of Deities...
And wondering as to what's waiting for us.. next day!
Events of the day lived
Flow once again as memory
In front of eyes- that screen keeps on moving..
And memories of my Mom! Telling me to
keep on meditating for the upliftment of their souls
A duty honestly and fully being done by me...
Limitations however keep staring back at me!

Sadness- Grief all getting transformed into words
Words that struggle,-
To manifest themselves here on paper..
I remember quite few of dead people even today..
Beautiful Pasts they all did have....
Stunned todays... kept raining on them all the days
A meaningless "Tomorrows" seemingly the mirages we heard of those Illusions take over my mind set...
I..now dead for a while
Unresponsive to what all happens around
Me... being told the next day itself..
The patient on your neighbouring bed
died last night..
No tears came out..
But in fact a bitter smile and I thought,
Oh! So! Deities finally decided.... he has had enough of it.

So walked out our own Charlie.
Building huge hospitals for all these – his own devotees
Caring for them,- touring villages on the time,
broken souls- broken bodies and living corpses....
Just drifting around all the time.
Doing whatever good he could think of
Motivating people to understand Reality of Life.
Ah! Yes! Of that Karma!
Kartiki I have an idea
of what really Karma said
It was that- that what motivated me
Taking of "hopes" as leaves of a tree nearby
and life itself as a tree- protecting us from the heat !
If you feed these poor less-blessed souls-
And if you still feel..
You're losing everything,-
Just remember that...
Trees do lose their leaves every year...
Still- They do stand tall...
And wait for better days to come..
That's what keeps me...
Moving on this road untired...
Caring for more less-blessed
Souls – giving them company
For... as long as I can do
This mission remains,-
An unending travel for me
How I wish,-

You would accompany me
In this lonely path...
We've to do a lot many
Things before we do go
To sleep yet again!
And look here – I would
Sum our this chat today...
In these words...
Here I am who is alive on facebook,
A thought that I read on the Raven-wolf Page
A short summation that was given...
Was something that was close to my thinking
During that youthful time
I, having stepped out of the college
Same things could have been or
Anyone in that age group
This guy Pranav- They say a Kashmiri
With lovable a wife a darling of his -
Lost contact with her...
I pulled out a Tarot Card...
Checking up what he desired utmost
When he was fine –
Devoting all the time... and..
Attending to those Annual Pilgrimages
Pranav seems to be saying
Simple things that make me smile
The Sunrise the Moon dancing their way in -
The wind whistling past and the Nature too coming alive

Kids laughing and music playing,
Butterflies twirling all around
And the way it all looked...
Makes my heart smile.
This is what brings happiness
This is where
My soul is at peace!
So the Psychiatric Hospitals
Directing efforts that are insufficient
That I do know...
But my share of work. I must do!
And yes Kartiki-

One more thing that struck me some time ago...
While travelling to reach here,
I was wondering about the various colures,-
That life really exudes,-
Through so many characters...
That we come across in our routine life.

Life is very beautiful. Even if just one 50 rupees note falls out from the pocket – a man does get upset – becomes nervous- starts looking out for it- apprehensive that it might have got lost. Such persons you must have seen plenty. And even after he is now past his fifties and having lived all the time in such state of mind- no change can be seen in him. He continues to behave in the same careless way as his routine remains unhinged as usual and you might say of that as a routine pattern. What a pity?

Essence of Life

And yes while walking along side this beach that ever thought of what exactly is the "**Essence of Life!**"I often wonder of it when I attempt to recollect – reflect on what all did take place on my own life – and in the life of others who came closer to me in this self-chosen travel of mine. True, God does bestow a beginning point for all of us to experience the 'real life' but the subsequent travel cannot be said to have taken place without any thing like our wilful contribution. Things going well or wrong,- we do have some role in that outcome. That is for sure, you can take it from me- Kartiki!

And if you do wish to ask me that what I think of this aspect- the true essence of day to day living, yes there is yet another phrase of CONSCIOUS Living which is meant for the people, who wish to live on a much higher plane than the millions of commoners that we see around us.

Life to me,- tells me to take... what that comes in- a day in our own stride- just like a Bus Conductor. Just think of his life, honey and you will understand what life percolates to the lower streams of human populace. For the Bus Conductor give a thought to what I am saying as a part of conscious living.

Every day, there are always- different –different types of passengers- but in reality not even one of them is someone whom we can think of as our own or ours! The daily journey-assumes a daily routine format- but in reality –we- ourselves through riding the bus – have no particular destination to go. Why – for that matter- all that money that is in the bag is also not ours. It is when we hand over,- all of it- at the end of our duty hours to the proper authorities.

It is then that we can consider that our duty for the day is perfectly over. That is all to it. So friends,- **"Life certainly is most beautiful"**. All that we have to do is to enjoy it to our own heart's content – so long as we are here. Even if we cannot take away or carry anything from here while departing once for all-it is far far better to attempt staying happily -for a while- in everyone's mind. That my dear lady, is true living or the true essence of living that one could be really proud of.

Chapter-27

The Hon'ble Court has given a complete hearing to all the concerned parties.

The Panvel Corporation Authorities simply maintained that, all they did was to pick him up... as he was wandering everywhere without any ideas whatsoever– but had not done anything violent or any objectionable act. It was not for them to say –if he truly was just an actor or a psychopath – that would be the responsibility of the Hospital authorities, who had been given a custody of the man for last 2-3 days as our registered Associate Social Organisation.

Hospital Authorities maintained that...in that short time, just nominal investigation could begin as a preliminary check-up of his existing mindset status. But there had been no instance of the man,-misbehaving in the hospital and as such-it would be possible to comment only after he completes a 30 days stay,- as per our norms..under observation of the Chief Doctor, who will decide the course of action to be followed in his context as to the treatment. Medical Reports– highlighted the extremely pleasant behaviour of the man with the school-going children and also with the Authorities of all the holy shrines with whom he had come in contact during his visits during the days of *'Mahashiv-Ratri'* festivities.

The Media reports as to "Charlie is Back", by the famous reporter Kartiki Madam of 'Soch TV' in fact, spoke well about the anectodes of Charlie's previous instances with Nanarao and his film studio and had been informed about the experimentation done by Nanarao and his Production Team for the film being made under their banner -captioned "Charlie is Back." In an innovative machine made by way of a brain wave of tampering ways Pranav's memory base with Charlie Chaplin's Artificial memory base created out of all gathered earlier pictures of Charlie Chaplin right from the period of Silent Era and subsequent Sound Movies. So as to save substantially on the movie production expenses. In a small mishap in the trial production Pranav the Actor from Kashmir got his brain damaged and he totally forgot his own identity and became totally ignorant and innocent just like a child without any memory. Any human right violation is also being separately ordered as the experimentation was totally illegal and in violence of the provisions of Human Rights Act. This Court instruct the relevant Human Rights Authorities to probe into the matter and also assess the damage done to the Actor by Nanarao and his team. The Actor can, at his will through his guardian file a rightful compensation claim against the Nanarao and his Production Team. Madam Kartiki is specially appointed on behalf of this Court to ensure that the Hospital Authority will comply with the demands of the representatives of Human Rights Administration. A separate legal action may be triggered by the Human Rights Group.

Dr. Shiv Har Trinetre's online application to act as the patients's guardian was not objected to by anyone and the 'Soch' media reports had in fact already posted the Man's Sensible Interview talk with their News Reporter Kartiki, who had made it a point to visit the Hospital, when she had received vital information of the happenings in Nanarao's Film City Studio. Nanarao's pleadings were thought as a lopsided perception of a vested interest and the experimentation conducted by him on a human being called for severe penalties and in fact an attractive down payment be worked out as a compensation to the actor-patient, who had been mal-treated and procedures of any pending Human Rights Violation and legal implications is to be looked into by a proper Government Authority. 'Soch' media too received a strict warning as to the Media's sense of irresponsibility that had come to light - when asked probing questions as to their varying statements all through the last week.

Kartiki and Dr. Shiv Har Trinetre with our Charlie posed for a group photograph with Dr. Ashish coming out of all this with flying colours for a cautious handling of a potentially explosive matter.

Good work of Dr. Shiv Har Trinetre was publicly lauded and lot many Social Organisations came out with Substantial Donations on CSR funding for the noble work being looked after by the Visionary Management of the upcoming Hospital. Madam Kartiki's services as a Reporter drew praise for her excellent approach towards ensuring perfect justice to the well meaning Charlie,- our patient now under discussion.

It was now a matter of public concerns as to whether Pranav who had been subjected to a Memory Base Infusion in to his mind by being fed into that machine, would be getting fully recovered as a earlier Pranav- the Kashmiri citizen or now born as a new Charlie under the influence of that machine?

Can the Doctors at this Psychiatric Hospital be able to get Pranav fully clear of the Charlie Memory Base or will have to live as the new Charlie incarnation because of the Memory Base infused in the Nanarao's fabricated machine. Or can he be restored as the normal Pranav that was before getting into the Machine and continue his good work under a new identity to be allotted to him.

Kartiki declared her intentions as to resign from 'Soch' Media and come out in support of Dr. Shiv Trinetre noble work as a full time Administrator complying with all the provisions of Human Right Violation Act.

Yet the question about whether at all Pranav would be once again the Pranav, his family knew about or will be compelled to live like the Charlie that he became in that machine?

? ? ? ? ? ?

Question Mark that remained unanswered.

That remained the solitary question on everyone's face as to the man leading a normal life. And yet another question that remained unanswered, whether his memory about his family in Kashmir returned to the status that was prior to the experimentation and yet another question as to what would be thought of as a rightful compensation for all the torture the ignorant innocent person had to undergo because

of these Dream Merchants obsessed with making money caring nothing about the law or the legal implications of the violations of clauses enacted for the protection of common people.

!!! My unexpected encounter with Jr. Charlie !!!

Jr. Charlie –he prefers to be known by that name – sat beside me and posed with all my other resident, inmate friends who were very quiet at the opportunity that came unannounced and in so unexpected a way.

After his socialising with all the fellow residents was over- Junior Charlie said to me, "Sir, I came to know that of late, you are here, staying in Snehsawali and have begun to write once again. I have an assignment that might interest you and so far as I'm concerned. I have already told one and all that, I cannot think of any other person to portray the Chaplin Character in English – The way Arvind sir can do." If at all, he says no or declines- it is only then that I will look out for someone else. It is true that, I have made some notes in Marathi, Hindi and English which he will be using as the core content and surely– he will be adding to it all – his own personal touches that would enrich the content from within –apart from stressing the main theme of "Laugh those problems / worries away and think only of how to improvise- on the opportunity that has come to us by way of God's Blessings". I smiled at his this outburst and thought of my own to date travel.

By the end of 2023- having ample time to pen –let me tell you guys, "a remarkable achievement was that, I had penned two more translations". Those also from Marathi to English, but the original Authors were sceptic about the recessionary trend still being around and had advised me not to risk launching them in 2024. Economy did start picking up, but I had to abide by the decision of the original writers, who were quite close to me.

Well against this back drop, I had been praying for a really good book which would withstand this recessionary trend and present my translation capacities in a different perspective.

One such quote comes to my mind

"you'll find that LIFE is still worthwhile - If you just smile!"

This quote –if you observe keenly– uses the future model- **"will"** in **"You'll-** which in fact, is a contraction of the phrase, you will!"

It emphasises the power of a positive outlook.

Here- One would realise that the adverb "verb" modifies the magical word "smile!"

As to English learners- This presents a fantastic opportunity to explore the intricate facets of the English Language,- that which became known as a global language spread word-wide.

A brief reflection on the Charlie Chaplin's Greatest Speech (*Annexure-1*) ever- from the Great Dictator becomes logical as its impact on creative minds pooling themselves together as volunteers in creation of a decent world.

A few days back, I was sitting in our In-house Temple of Snehsawali Care Centre, and was engaged in Meditation – Having had a reasonably good response to my earlier 5 published transliterations- (2 from English to Marathi, 2 from Marathi to English and 1 from English to Kannada) and each of these books, despite being just translations did get a honourable break-even despite the recession in the market around,- due to CORONA hit economy was thought of as an impediment to sales of the books.

A quote that I keep remembering all the time,- one of that Great Soul !

> *"My pain may be the reason*
> *for somebody's laugh.*
> *But my laugh must never be*
> *the reason for somebody's pain!"*
>
> **..Charlie Chaplin.**

Prof. Arvind Kulkarni of Ex-MGM JNEC and Snehasawali Care Centre, Beed bypass, Chatrapati Sambhajinagar (Aurangabad-India), who has related the fantasy presented by our Jr. Charlie about the yesteryear Superstar ***Charlie Chaplin*** coming to India to finish his incomplete mission of enlightening the masses through pure entertainment and self imagined events. Details about my personal intimacies with our own Jr. Charlie, - a rural base Marathi Actor shall figure in the Annexure- Chapter that follows the original version of our own Jr. Charlie. Both the Charlie did take help of associate staff in underscoring a magnificent journey of pure bliss, a level lived by them. That story is for more vital- so let's hop on to the Journey of Jr. Charlie... possessed by the Senior Charlie Chaplin,-acknowledged worldwide.

Jr. Charlie entered and an un-thought of "Applause" by hands clapping with the people in auditorium getting up and standing up, started as he entered the stage on the evergreen carpet of our Cultural Hall. These were about 130 or so people cheering the upcoming Philosophical and yet a

Comedian Artist who had made a name for himself devoting all of his talents, and resources but the backing of his wife acting as a cheering- something remaining of Fairy- Tale Companion. They had, by now- in the last few years- out of the stage shows had managed to clear all the earlier loans and were looking out for coming up with ideas of instituting a Charlie Chaplin Publication house that would direct their entire earnings to the world of less blessed through various social organisations with a track record of really Transparent Administration and to Chaplin along with his around 130 followers spread out all over *Marathwada* and some bordering districts from other regions of Maharashtra would be a strength as rural backup force of volunteers helping our Sr. Citizens or purely dependent people with no economic support. Volunteer force would be backing health and healing programs of reputed NGO's operating in Health Care Segment-like our own Snehsawali Care Centre.

The function itself was a great success and this additional Jr. Chaplin touch got him a backing to support his cause. The morale of Jr. Charlie group got shot up high by this appreciation by upcoming starts of Marathi Literaturers. The portrait on the page 13 previously brings out the approach aspect of the feelings lived by the original Charlie Chaplin.

Jr. Chaplin suddenly spoke upto the Audience "A dark past doesn't mean you can't have a brighter future, look forward to new chapters and most importantly a NEW YOU! "

OUR VISION & MISSION

Various Art forms, Training, Mentoring of famous artists in the country and abroad for artists to progress in the field of art making proper prepartions to present art around the world - trying to make progress keeping the family and themselves. Safe and also getting the artists an authorized groups status and solo commercial entertainments social awarness and advertising license by the Govt. of India and connecting them to various business streams. We are trying to provide promotion and employment throught digital Website and Other Social Media Tools.

We are also planning a seperate weekly digital (social media) and print magazine for artists by the foundation that will provide only positive reviews of weekly happenings related to artists and provide them with event opportunities. So this foundation magazine will be very importants to provide employment for all the artists and make maximum use of if for the sustainance of their families.

President	Vice President	Secretary
Somnath S. Swabhavane	Sumeet Pandit	Rupali S. Swabhavane
(Junior Charlie)	(Social Work)	Cell. : 9881843202
Cell. : 9595869370	Cell. : 7588928822	

• Members •
Jyoti Deval, Puja Pandit, Kalpesh Pandit, Rushikesh Swabhavane

FOUNDATION ACTIVITIES

135 JUNIOR CHARLIES ARTISTS, A MUSICAL MONOLOGUE

135 Junior Charlie Creating Artists and making them self sufficient in the field of Art.

B-Positive Monologue Musical street play.

CHARILI IS BACK

Charlie is Back (English, Hindi & Marathi Novel Writing and Publishing puprose.

A Novel - Travelling from JammuKashmit to Mumbai, through Hindi / English / Marthi Composition titled "Charilie is Back !! film secor, Artist Sector, Business Sector, Tourism Sector. A Novel about the human psyche and the importance of being 'happy' in the life "Charlie is Back" will be written and published with a view for Distribution accross India and Globally as well.
Blue Rose One, Stories Matter New Delhi, & London

Social Infection Drama

The purpose of producing Comidy - 2 Act Play" is to put forward a Social positive prospective - that presents the pain of struggling familesi and artists in Mumbai in the form of entertainment based on the social infection drama, the side effects and mosuse of the social Media
Author : Hansini Uchit, Washim

THE JR. CHARLIE FOUNDATION
Present a
Two Act Hilarious Comedy Play
"Little By Little - But All Three Crazy"
Author : Sumit Taur Director : Shankar Thube

Cast : Gauri Aher, Shreya Ughade,
Saurabh Padmakar, Shrikrishna Kaudgaonkar
Shankar Thube Arun Tupe Ajay Dehade

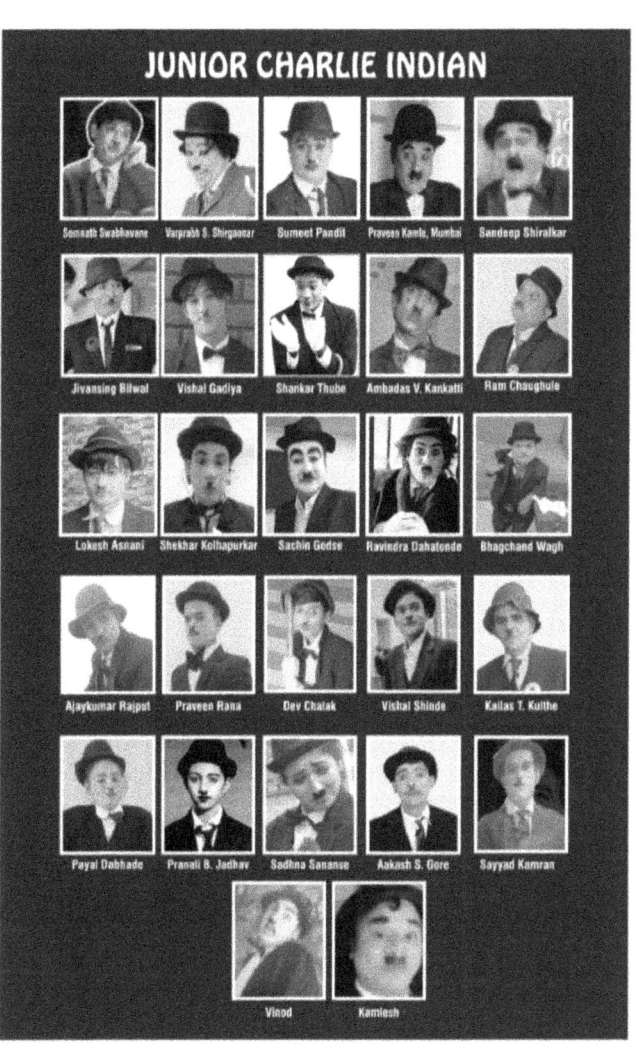

"Charlie is Back"

Special Thanks...

Publication	:	**Blue Rose Publishers.**
Language Translator	:	**Prof. Arvind Kulkarni.**
Typist	:	***Muhurt Creation –*** **Balaji R. Tak,** **Satish Munge.** ***Arjun Arts –*** **Arjun R. Mishra.**
Cover & Sketch Artist	:	**Ramesh Tagad,** **Sanjivani B. Tak,** **Nilesh B. Gavale.**

www.ingramcontent.com/pod-product-compliance
Lightning Source LLC
LaVergne TN
LVHW061547070526
838199LV00077B/6940